Exploring Genesis: A Theolog Journey

MW00877817

Jim Russo

profjim@email.com

Published by Deo Gratias, LLC – Detroit, MI

Printed and bound in the United States of America

First Printing

Table of Contents

1 <u>About the author</u>

Jim Russo had a conversion experience while studying computer science in his first year of college which led him to study instead for the Catholic priesthood under the tutelage of several world-class theologians at both college and graduate

seminary. When he was a student in graduate seminary where he received his master's degree in theology, Jim had the opportunity to study in Israel and Rome.

While in the seminary, Jim met with notables such as Monsignor Clem Kern, Ceasar Chavez, Eli Weisel, Pope John Paul II, and Mother Teresa.

Jim eventually left the seminary after meeting a person he would later marry and have children with. Recently retired from a career in computer science which spanned nearly 40 years, Jim and his wife Beth, both devout Christians, cherish spending time with their family, friends and enjoy traveling.

1.1 Dedication

Given that this is my first and perhaps my only book, I dedicate this book to my cherished family and friends, both the living and the dearly departed. They have offered support which motivated me in times of trial, brought me tremendous satisfaction, and have all taught me the meaning of love.

I offer most profound gratitude to the Divine, The Author of Space and Time, Who continues to love 'a wretch like me' without measure, providing His Grace beyond comprehension.

2 <u>Introduction</u>

I invite you on a journey to explore the Book of Genesis through a theologically and scientifically informed lens. I must emphasize that my intent is not to disparage or belittle the views held by Fundamentalists. Rather, I seek to present their perspective with accuracy and fairness while simultaneously offering an alternate viewpoint.

Let me clarify that my purpose is not to undermine the sacredness of Scripture or challenge its divine inspiration. On the contrary, I firmly believe in the Word of God, acknowledging its profound impact on countless lives throughout history. However, I also acknowledge that the Bible, though divinely inspired, was penned by human authors who may have introduced some inconsistencies.

Throughout this text, I will refrain from trying to establish the Bible's biblical authority, a concept commonly known as Sola Scriptura, which Evangelicals uphold as a rejection of certain Catholic doctrines. I aim to foster understanding and mutual respect among all readers, regardless of their religious background.

Drawing upon my education and experiences studying in various theological institutions, including Sacred Heart Minor Seminary, Saint John's Major Seminary, the Ecumenical Institute for Advanced Theological Studies in Tantur, Israel, and the Pontifical Biblical Institute in Rome, I will primarily focus on the Book of Genesis.

Jesus referred to Genesis in both Matthew 24:37-39 and Luke 17:26-27. However, reading these references in the broader context of Scripture, Jesus' purpose to quote from Genesis was not to endorse the historicity of Genesis but instead to support profound spiritual lessons.

Central to my perspective is Romans 10:13-14, which highlights that salvation comes from our personal belief in Jesus Christ as Lord and Savior, rather than our specific interpretations of Genesis or the rest of Scripture. We must recognize the Gospel's central message and not allow differences in scriptural interpretations to divide us.

It is also essential to acknowledge that the majority view in both theology and science should not dictate our beliefs. While I present a more mainstream theological and scientific explanation of Genesis, I believe that the Bible is infallible in matters of faith and morals; although, certainly not intended to be either a book of science or history.

Rather than solely focusing on accepting the Genesis account as a historical narrative, I encourage readers to recognize the greatness and glory of God. He is the Creator of the Universe, present at its inception, and intimately aware of each person's existence. God's omnipotence ensures that every moment is purposeful, including the writing of this book and your reading of it.

Though I believe in evolution, I firmly believe that we are not here by random chance. Instead, I affirm that God remains in control of His creation, guiding its course with divine wisdom and purpose.

I write this text as a devoted Christian who wholeheartedly believes in the redemptive power of Jesus Christ. His sacrifice on the cross is a testament to the immense love of God for humanity. I hope that this exploration of Genesis will inspire readers to seek a deeper understanding of God's Word and draw closer to the divine truth it contains. Let us journey together with open minds, mutual respect, and a shared pursuit of spiritual growth.

2.1 Purpose and scope of this book

If I agreed with the Creationist and Fundamentalist view, there would be no need for me to write this book. I have been ruminating about the thoughts which I hope to express in this book for most of my adult life; however, after watching the debate between Bill Nye and Ken Ham on YouTube[i], I felt compelled to write what follows.

The Fundamentalist view of the Bible often conflicts with the findings of modern science due to various reasons. It's important to note that not all Christians or religious individuals hold Fundamentalist views, and many Christians find ways to reconcile their faith with science. However, here are some reasons why aspects of the Fundamentalist view of the Bible may conflict with science:

1. Fundamentalists often interpret the Bible literally, which can lead to conflicts with scientific evidence that contradicts literal readings of certain passages, such as the creation account in Genesis.

2. Some Fundamentalists adhere to the belief in a young Earth, which rejects the scientific consensus on the age of the Earth, estimated to be around 4.5 billion years old based on geological evidence.

3. Many Fundamentalists reject the theory of evolution, which is widely supported by scientific evidence and is the cornerstone of modern biology.

4. Nearly all Fundamentalists promote the idea of a global flood as described in the Bible, which conflicts with the overwhelming evidence in geology and other fields indicating that no such global flood occurred.

5. The belief in the inerrancy and infallibility of the Bible can create conflicts with scientific findings that challenge certain historical or cosmological events as depicted in the Bible.

6. The Fundamentalist view often attributes natural phenomena solely to supernatural causation, which hinders the pursuit of scientific explanations and understanding of natural processes.

7. The literal interpretation of the creation account in Genesis conflicts with the scientific understanding of human evolution and the common ancestry of all living beings.

8. The Bible's cosmological passages are significantly at odds with modern scientific theories about the origin and structure of the universe.

It's important to reiterate that not all Christians or religious individuals interpret the Bible in a Fundamentalist way, and many religious communities find harmony between their faith and scientific understanding by adopting different approaches to biblical interpretation. The conflict between science and religion often arises when religious texts are taken as literal and scientific findings are dismissed or ignored. However, many believers accept scientific discoveries and view them as complementary to their faith.

2.2 Acknowledging the theological and scientific tension

The study of Genesis, the foundational book of the Bible, has long been a subject of both theological and scientific scrutiny. As we embark on this theological and scientific journey to explore the narratives of Genesis, it is crucial to recognize and acknowledge the inherent tensions that arise when these two disciplines intersect. Examination of the book of Genesis requires a balanced and respectful approach to understanding the text.

Genesis holds significant theological importance for various religious traditions. As believers hold this text as divinely inspired and authoritative, tensions may arise when scientific findings seemingly challenge literal interpretations of the creation narratives or other events.

One of the most prominent theological tensions revolves around the compatibility of the Genesis creation accounts with the scientific view of cosmology and the theory of evolution. Addressing these tensions requires a nuanced understanding of biblical hermeneutics and scientific theories.

Some of the points of tension are the following:

Genesis portrays Adam and Eve as the first human beings, while scientific evidence points to a more complex evolutionary history. Reconciling these differing perspectives necessitates careful theological reflections.

Scientific inquiry relies on observable evidence and testable hypotheses. When examining Genesis narratives, discrepancies with established scientific data on cosmology, geology, and biology may arise.

Scientific investigation generally adheres to methodological naturalism, focusing on natural causes and processes. This can lead to tensions when discussing supernatural events described in Genesis, such as miracles or divine interventions.

Assessing the historical accuracy of Genesis events, such as the global flood, presents challenges when comparing biblical accounts with archaeological and geological records.

Acknowledging the complexities of theological and scientific investigations requires humility and open-mindedness. Both disciplines have their strengths and limitations, and recognizing these helps cultivate a respectful dialogue.

Understanding the various literary forms employed in Genesis, such as myth, poetry, and historical narrative, helps interpret the text more faithfully. Distinguishing between theological truths and historical facts is essential to avoid unnecessary conflicts.

Viewing theological and scientific perspectives as complementary rather than contradictory can lead to a more harmonious engagement with Genesis. Appreciating the different insights each discipline provides enriches our understanding of the text's multidimensional nature.

Embracing historical-critical methods allows scholars to explore the historical context, literary sources, and authorship of Genesis while respecting its theological significance.

Employing theological hermeneutics aids in discerning the enduring theological truths conveyed in Genesis while acknowledging the cultural and historical distance between the text and contemporary readers.

Engaging with scientific findings requires integrity in understanding and representing scientific theories accurately. Misrepresenting scientific evidence can lead to further tensions and hinder productive dialogue.

Recognizing the diverse domains of theology and science enables us to appreciate the richness of knowledge and promote interdisciplinary discussions. Seeking unity amid diversity encourages holistic learning.

Acknowledging the theological and scientific tensions in the interpretation of Genesis is an essential first step in our journey. Embracing a humble and open-minded approach, recognizing the distinct contributions of each discipline, and seeking common ground in our pursuit of understanding will pave the way for a meaningful exploration of the theological and scientific aspects of Genesis. As we move forward, we will delve deeper into specific theological and scientific points, seeking to find harmony between these two vital dimensions of human inquiry.

2.3 Importance of an integrated approach to Genesis

Genesis, as the foundational book of the Bible, holds profound significance for religious faith, cultural heritage, and human understanding of our origins. Throughout history, interpretations of Genesis have often been polarized between theological and scientific perspectives. It is important to adopt an integrated approach to Genesis—one that embraces both theological and scientific insights. By recognizing the complementary nature of these disciplines, we can navigate the complexities of the text with greater nuance and arrive at a more comprehensive understanding of its message.

Theological and scientific truths need not be seen as mutually exclusive. Embracing an integrated approach allows us to appreciate the beauty and complexity of the natural world while exploring the profound theological insights within Genesis.

By acknowledging the natural world as God's creation, an integrated approach reinforces the notion that divine revelation can be discerned both through Scripture and through the study of nature.

Understanding the historical context of Genesis enables us to grasp the text's original intent and the cultural milieu in which it was written. This context is essential for interpreting the text responsibly and avoiding anachronistic interpretations.

An integrated approach recognizes that ancient cosmology and symbolic language were common literary devices in the ancient Near East. Grasping these elements enriches our understanding of the theological messages conveyed in the text.

An integrated approach enables us to appreciate Genesis' portrayal of God's attributes and divine nature. Exploring the theological truths about God fosters a deeper understanding of the divine-human relationship.

Genesis offers profound ethical insights into human behavior, social responsibility, and justice. Integrating these moral teachings into our lives enhances our ethical understanding and personal growth.

An integrated approach embraces scientific findings about the natural world, from cosmology to evolutionary biology. This fosters an appreciation for the wonders of creation and the ongoing pursuit of knowledge.

Recognizing that Genesis employs ancient cosmological language does not diminish the theological significance of creation. Rather, it invites us to discern the theological message within the ancient framework.

An integrated approach fosters productive dialogue between theologians and scientists, breaking down barriers that may hinder communication and collaboration.

Engaging in interdisciplinary dialogue brings diverse insights, fostering a more comprehensive and enriched understanding of Genesis and its implications for contemporary life.

An integrated approach reminds us of the limitations of human knowledge and the humility required in approaching sacred texts and scientific inquiries.

Some aspects of Genesis may remain mysterious or beyond human comprehension. An integrated approach encourages us to embrace these mysteries and respect the boundaries of knowledge.

An integrated approach to Genesis brings together the richness of theology and the discoveries of science. Recognizing the unity of truth and appreciating the distinct contributions of both disciplines allows us to delve into Genesis with humility and openness. By integrating theological insights, historical context, scientific knowledge, and interdisciplinary dialogue, we can glean a deeper and more holistic understanding of Genesis, appreciating its enduring relevance in guiding our understanding of the divine, the human condition, and our place within the natural world.

2.4 Definition of terms

"Creationists" and "Fundamentalist Christians" are terms that often overlap, but they refer to distinct concepts within the context of religious beliefs, particularly in relation to the origin of life and the interpretation of religious texts. Here's a breakdown of the differences between the two:

Creationists:

Creationism is a belief system that holds that the universe, Earth, and all life forms were created by a divine being or beings, and that this creation process aligns with religious texts such as the Bible. Creationists reject the idea of purely naturalistic explanations for the origin of life and the diversity of species, advocating instead for a supernatural explanation involving a higher power. Creationism can encompass various interpretations, including:

>**Young Earth Creationism:** This subset of creationism holds that the Earth and the universe were created relatively recently (usually within a few thousand years) and is often based on a literal interpretation of the Bible's creation account in the book of Genesis.

>**Old Earth Creationism:** Some creationists accept that the Earth is much older than a few thousand years, but still attribute its creation to a divine source. They often integrate scientific theories about the age of the Earth with their religious beliefs.

>**Intelligent Design:** While not always synonymous with creationism, proponents of intelligent design argue that certain features of the natural world are best explained by an intelligent cause rather than purely natural processes.

This idea doesn't always specify the nature of the intelligent designer, but it's often associated with religious viewpoints.

Fundamentalist Christians:

Fundamentalism is an approach to religion that emphasizes the strict adherence to a set of core beliefs, often considered "fundamental" to the faith. Fundamentalist Christians are those who hold to a literal interpretation of their sacred texts, particularly the Bible, and resist or reject interpretations that depart from their understanding of these texts. They often take a strong stance on doctrinal purity and may be resistant to adapting their beliefs to accommodate modern scientific theories or cultural changes.

Fundamentalist Christians can encompass a range of theological and social beliefs beyond just creationism, including attitudes toward gender roles, morality, and social issues. Not all fundamentalist Christians are strictly creationist, but many do hold creationist views due to their literal interpretation of Genesis and other relevant biblical passages.

"Creationists" primarily focus on the belief that a divine being or beings played a direct role in the origin of life and the universe, while "Fundamentalist Christians" emphasize strict adherence to traditional religious teachings and a literal interpretation of sacred texts. Creationism is often one component of the broader belief system held by many fundamentalist Christians.

3 Approaches to Scriptural Study

3.1 Overview

Scriptural study is a foundational practice within various religious traditions, allowing adherents to delve deeper into the sacred texts and gain insights into their beliefs and doctrines. Creationists, Fundamentalists, and Catholics each approach this study with distinctive methodologies and tools, reflecting their unique theological perspectives and goals. While there are some intersections in the tools employed, there are also notable divergences that arise from differences in interpretation and theological emphasis.

Creationists, who adhere to the belief in a literal interpretation of the Bible's account of creation, often employ tools that prioritize harmonizing scientific evidence with their scriptural convictions. They may utilize concordances, which provide exhaustive lists of every occurrence of a specific word in the Bible, to trace references to creation and related themes throughout the text. Additionally, Creationists may lean on commentaries that align with their viewpoint, such as those authored by young-earth creationists, to provide insights and explanations that reinforce their beliefs. Prominent figures like Henry Morris[ii] and Ken Ham[iii] have written extensively on this topic, offering works like "The Genesis Flood"[iv] and "The Answers Book,"[v] which provide creationist perspectives on geological and cosmological matters.

Fundamentalists, often associated with strict adherence to the core tenets of a religious tradition, approach scriptural study with an emphasis on textual analysis and contextual understanding. They frequently utilize tools such as interlinear Bibles, which display the original language text alongside a word-for-word translation, enabling them to delve into linguistic nuances and original meanings. Cross-referencing tools like biblical concordances and lexicons assist Fundamentalists in exploring how key terms are used in various contexts throughout the Scriptures. Furthermore, they may engage with historical commentaries from theologians like John Calvin or Jonathan Edwards, seeking insights that align with their theological convictions while also delving into the historical context of biblical passages.

Catholics, with a rich tradition of ecclesiastical authority and doctrinal interpretation, bring a distinctive approach to scriptural study. They emphasize the role of the Magisterium—the teaching authority of the Church—in guiding the interpretation of Scripture. Catholics often use tools like the Catechism of the Catholic Church[vi] to understand how official Church teachings relate to specific passages. The use of exegetical resources, such as the Navarre Bible[vii]series, combines commentary from Church Fathers, saints, and modern scholars, facilitating a multifaceted interpretation that draws from both tradition and contemporary scholarship. The Liturgy of the Hours, a structured cycle of daily prayers based on Scripture, offers Catholics a way to engage with the Word of God regularly in a communal and liturgical context.

While there are commonalities across these approaches, divergences also arise. Creationists' emphasis on a literal interpretation of creation narratives may diverge significantly from Catholic and Fundamentalist allegorical or symbolic readings. Fundamentalists' rigorous linguistic analysis differs from the more tradition-centered Catholic approach that integrates Church authority and historical context. Despite these differences, it's worth noting that all three groups value scriptural study as a means of deepening their faith and understanding, showcasing the diverse ways in which religious traditions engage with their sacred texts.

3.2 Creationist Approach

3.2.1 Bible as ultimate source of truth

From a Creationist perspective, the study of Scripture is approached with reverence and a belief in its divine inspiration. Creationists view the Bible as the ultimate source of truth, guiding their understanding of the world's origins, purpose, and the principles by which they live their lives. The process of studying Scripture involves careful examination of the text, considering its historical and cultural contexts, linguistic nuances, and theological teachings.

At the core of Creationist interpretation lies a commitment to a literal understanding of the biblical text. This involves taking the words of the Bible at face value, believing that they convey historical and scientific truths. One foundational Creationist belief is the doctrine of biblical inerrancy, which holds that the Bible is without error in all its teachings. This doctrine guides the Creationist approach to studying Scripture and informs their understanding of the world's creation as outlined in the Book of Genesis.

Genesis 1 and 2 are of paramount importance to Creationists, as these chapters detail the account of creation. Creationists often emphasize the six-day creation narrative, wherein God creates the universe, Earth, and all living creatures in six literal days. Genesis 1:1 sets the stage with the famous words, "In the beginning, God created the heavens and the earth." This verse forms the foundation of the Creationist belief in God as the ultimate Creator of all things.

When studying the account of creation, Creationists consider the context in which Genesis was written. They emphasize that the author, likely Moses, was inspired by God to record a historical and accurate account of the world's origins. By examining the original Hebrew text, linguistic nuances, and the cultural milieu of the time, Creationists seek to gain a deeper understanding of the intended meaning of the text.

Creationist study of Scripture is also influenced by the principle of harmonization, wherein seemingly contradictory passages within the Bible are reconciled to form a coherent theological framework. This approach leads Creationists to interpret other portions of Scripture, such as the genealogies in Genesis and the Flood narrative, as historical events that align with the account of creation.

From a Creationist perspective, the study of Scripture involves a literal interpretation of the Bible as the inspired and inerrant Word of God. This approach informs their understanding of the world's creation, the purpose of humanity, and the guiding principles for their lives. Genesis 1 and 2, particularly the six-day creation narrative, hold a central place in Creationist beliefs, and the study of these chapters is conducted with a commitment to understanding the text's historical, linguistic, and theological contexts. Through this lens, Creationists find assurance in their understanding of the origins of the universe and the role of humanity as divinely created beings.

3.2.2 Perspective on "Historical History" and "Observational History"

From a Creationist perspective, the distinction between "Historical History"[viii] and "Observational History"[ix] is rooted in their understanding of the biblical narrative and the reliability of

Scripture as a historical record. Creationists emphasize that the events described in the Bible, especially those in the early chapters of Genesis, are not merely allegorical or symbolic, but rather represent actual historical occurrences. This leads to a framework in which "Historical History" pertains to events recorded in the Bible's historical accounts, while "Observational History" encompasses recorded human history.

Creationists point to passages like Genesis 1-11 as "Historical History," detailing the creation of the universe, the fall of humanity, the global flood, and the dispersion at the Tower of Babel. These narratives are regarded as factual accounts of past events that shaped the course of human history. For instance, Genesis 11:1-9 describes the confusion of languages at the Tower of Babel, which Creationists understand as the origin of diverse languages and cultures. The biblical record provides a framework for understanding "Historical History" and its impact on humanity's development.

Creationists argue that "Observational History" is subject to limitations and biases, as historical events beyond a certain point cannot be directly observed or tested. They suggest that assumptions and interpretations can influence how historical events are understood. Creationists often maintain that the Bible offers a reliable historical framework, serving as a benchmark for evaluating and understanding "Observational History."

From a Fundamentalist perspective, the distinction between "Historical History" and "Observational History" aligns with their belief in the inerrancy and reliability of the biblical record. Fundamentalists view the Bible as a comprehensive source of historical truth, encompassing both the "Historical History" of biblical events and the "Observational History" of recorded human history.

Fundamentalists emphasize that the historical narratives in the Bible, such as the accounts of creation, the patriarchs, and the nation of Israel, provide an accurate and reliable record of past events. These narratives are considered to be historical facts rather than allegories or myths. For instance, Genesis 1-2 is interpreted as "Historical History," describing the creation of the world in six literal days.

In contrast, "Observational History" includes historical records beyond the scope of biblical narratives, often beginning with events that can be observed and recorded through human documentation. Fundamentalists assert that the Bible's historical accuracy sets a standard for evaluating other historical records and events. They argue that the biblical framework provides a coherent context for understanding human history, allowing for a more meaningful interpretation of "Observational History."

The distinction between "Historical History" and "Observational History" reflects the Creationist and Fundamentalist commitment to understanding the past within the context of a biblical worldview. Both perspectives regard the Bible as a reliable source of historical truth, shaping their interpretations of events and the development of human history. This distinction underscores the significance of the biblical record as a foundational guide for evaluating and understanding the complexities of human history.

3.2.3 Perspective on "Historical science" and "Observational science"

From a Creationist perspective, the distinction between "Historical Science"[x] and "Observational Science"[xi] is a foundational aspect of how they approach scientific inquiry and understanding of the past. Creationists emphasize the importance of distinguishing between observational science, which deals with directly observable and repeatable phenomena, and historical science, which involves interpreting past events that are not directly observable in the present.

Creationists argue that while observational science, such as laboratory experiments and current observations, can provide reliable data, historical science relies on assumptions and interpretations that may be influenced by worldviews. They often refer to passages like Genesis 1, which describe the creation of the universe, as a historical record and foundational truth. Creationists contend that interpretations of past events should align with the biblical account, as it offers a reliable framework for understanding the origin and history of the world.

One of the examples Creationists often point to is the field of paleontology. They assert that while fossils and rock layers are observable in the present, the interpretation of the past based on these observations is subject to various assumptions. Creationists suggest that alternative interpretations, informed by the biblical timeline, can offer a different understanding of the history of life on Earth. They emphasize that historical science involves making assumptions about unobservable past events, and these assumptions can be influenced by one's worldview.

From a Fundamentalist perspective, the distinction between "Historical Science" and "Observational Science" reflects their belief in the importance of understanding scientific endeavors within a biblical framework. Fundamentalists often emphasize the limitations of human knowledge when it comes to interpreting events that occurred in the distant past. They contend that while observational science, characterized by empirical observations and experiments, is valuable for understanding present phenomena, historical science involves making assumptions about unobservable past events.

Fundamentalists draw attention to passages in Scripture that provide a historical account of creation, such as Genesis 1-2. They view these narratives as the ultimate authority for understanding the origins of the universe and the Earth. Fundamentalists argue that the principles of observational science, which rely on testable and repeatable experiments, are consistent with a biblical worldview and can provide valuable insights into the functioning of the natural world.

When considering topics like the age of the Earth or the history of life on Earth, Fundamentalists often stress the role of assumptions and interpretations in historical science. They highlight that different assumptions can lead to different conclusions, and these assumptions may be influenced by one's worldview or philosophical beliefs. While recognizing the importance of scientific inquiry, Fundamentalists prioritize aligning interpretations of historical science with the teachings of Scripture.

Both the Creationist and Fundamentalist perspectives on "Historical Science" and "Observational Science" reflect their commitment to understanding the past within a biblical framework. While acknowledging the value of observational science for understanding present phenomena, both perspectives emphasize the influence of assumptions and interpretations in historical science. These distinctions underscore the broader implications of worldviews and the importance of aligning scientific understandings with faith-based perspectives on the origin and history of the universe.

3.2.4 "Historical" and "Observational" Perspectives in a Nutshell

The distinction between "Historical" and "Observational" perspectives holds profound significance within the frameworks of Creationism and Fundamentalism, offering insights into how these perspectives approach the interpretation of past events and the understanding of historical truth. Both viewpoints share a commitment to the reliability of Scripture but diverge in their approach to interpreting historical and observational data.

From a Creationist standpoint, the distinction between "Historical" and "Observational" perspectives is grounded in a deep reverence for the biblical text as a comprehensive source of historical and spiritual truth. Creationists maintain that the Bible presents "Historical" narratives that convey factual accounts of events shaping humanity's origins and development. These narratives, such as the creation of the world in six days (Genesis 1) or the worldwide flood (Genesis 6-9), are considered historical realities that have impacted the course of human history.

Genesis 1, for instance, is regarded as a "Historical" account of the creation of the universe. Creationists often emphasize the literal interpretation of the six-day creation narrative, asserting that God's creative acts were accomplished in distinct periods. The events recorded in this passage are understood as foundational truths that shape the understanding of the origin of all things.

In contrast, "Observational" perspectives encompass events that have occurred since the time of direct human observation and record-keeping. While Creationists acknowledge the value of observational science, they emphasize that interpreting past events beyond human memory requires the application of assumptions and worldview considerations. Creationists often highlight that interpretations of "Observational" data can be influenced by one's understanding of "Historical" events as recorded in Scripture. Geological formations, fossil records, and historical documents can be assessed within this framework to align with a biblical worldview.

Fundamentalists share a similar reverence for the Bible's historical accuracy and theological authority. They view the "Historical" narratives in Scripture, such as the lives of patriarchs and events leading up to the life of Christ, as factual accounts of past events. These narratives offer insights into the character of God, the human condition, and the unfolding of God's redemptive plan.

For instance, the "Historical" account of Abraham's willingness to offer Isaac as a sacrifice (Genesis 22) is seen as a profound demonstration of faith and obedience. Fundamentalists hold that these events are not allegorical but are grounded in historical reality, providing moral and spiritual lessons for believers.

"Observational" perspectives, on the other hand, pertain to historical records and events that are recorded by humans and observed in the course of human history. While acknowledging the limitations of historical records and the potential for bias, Fundamentalists prioritize the Bible's role as a guide for interpreting "Observational" data. They hold that the "Historical" accounts in Scripture establish a context for understanding and interpreting "Observational" history, providing a framework through which to discern the development of human civilization and societies.

The distinction between "Historical" and "Observational" perspectives is a pivotal consideration within Creationism and

Fundamentalism. While both perspectives emphasize the authority of the Bible, they approach historical events and recorded data through the lens of scriptural teachings and foundational truths. These perspectives underscore the complexities of interpreting the past and highlight the importance of aligning historical understanding with faithful adherence to biblical teachings.

Simply stated, Creationists rely on the Bible as a historic fact and scientific fact since they were not there to observe it.

3.3 Fundamentalist Approach

3.3.1 Sola Scriptura

From a Fundamentalist perspective, the study of Scripture is approached with unwavering dedication to its divine authority and infallibility. Fundamentalists regard the Bible as the inerrant and inspired Word of God, serving as the ultimate guide for faith and practice. The process of studying Scripture involves meticulous examination of its text, historical context, linguistic nuances, and theological teachings, all with the aim of understanding and applying its timeless truths to contemporary life.

Central to the Fundamentalist approach is the doctrine of biblical literalism. This entails interpreting the Bible in its most straightforward and natural sense, taking the words as they are written. Fundamentalists believe that the biblical authors were divinely guided and that the text itself is clear and understandable to those who approach it with sincerity and humility.

A key principle in Fundamentalist hermeneutics is the principle of Sola Scriptura, emphasizing Scripture as the ultimate authority over tradition, human reasoning, and personal experience. This principle is rooted in passages such as 2 Timothy 3:16-17, which asserts that all Scripture is "God-breathed" and profitable for teaching, reproof, correction, and training in righteousness.

When studying Scripture, Fundamentalists prioritize the historical and cultural context in which each book was written. Understanding the cultural norms, linguistic nuances, and historical background helps to illuminate the intended meaning of the text. This approach enables Fundamentalists to grasp the timeless truths conveyed within the context of the original audience.

For instance, when studying the account of creation in Genesis, Fundamentalists emphasize a literal interpretation of the six-day creation narrative. They point to passages like Exodus 20:11, where the Sabbath commandment connects the six days of creation to a literal week. This reinforces the belief that God created the universe in six literal days.

Fundamentalists also engage in textual analysis, comparing Scripture with Scripture to harmonize seemingly contradictory passages. This practice aligns with their conviction that the Bible is consistent and coherent in its teachings. By cross-referencing related verses and passages, they strive to form a unified understanding of God's revelation.

From a Fundamentalist perspective, the study of Scripture is characterized by an unwavering commitment to its divine inspiration, authority, and infallibility. Biblical literalism, the principle of Sola Scriptura, and contextual analysis are foundational to their hermeneutical approach. Through the diligent study of the text and reliance on the Holy Spirit's guidance, Fundamentalists seek to uncover the unchanging truths contained within the Bible and apply them to their lives in a manner that aligns with their understanding of God's intended message.

3.3.2 Fundamentalist Scriptural Resources

Fundamentalists engage in scriptural study with a deep commitment to the foundational doctrines and core tenets of their religious tradition. Their approach is characterized by a rigorous focus on the text of the Bible and a desire to extract the original meaning of the passages. To aid in their quest for scriptural understanding, Fundamentalists employ a variety of tools and resources that facilitate an in-depth examination of the text, linguistic nuances, and historical context.

One of the central tools used by Fundamentalists is the interlinear Bible. This resource presents the original language text (such as Hebrew or Greek) alongside a word-for-word translation, allowing scholars to delve into the intricacies of the languages and analyze the precise meanings of words and phrases. For instance, the "Interlinear Bible: Hebrew-Greek-English"[xii] provides a direct line of sight into the linguistic elements of the Bible, enabling Fundamentalists to better understand the underlying nuances of the original text.

Cross-referencing tools are also vital for Fundamentalist scriptural study. Biblical concordances, such as Strong's Concordance[xiii], enable individuals to locate every occurrence of a specific word or phrase in the Bible. This aids in comprehending how key terms are used across various contexts, contributing to a more holistic interpretation. Strong's Concordance, with its exhaustive index of every word in the King James Version of the Bible, serves as a reliable resource for Fundamentalists to explore the textual interconnections within the Scripture.

Lexicons are indispensable resources for Fundamentalist scholars seeking to understand the meanings of words in their original languages. The "Vine's Complete Expository Dictionary of Old and New Testament Words"[xiv] is a widely used lexicon that provides detailed explanations of biblical terms and their usage, helping to uncover the rich semantic range of words within their cultural and historical contexts. This tool enables Fundamentalists to conduct word studies and discern the subtle shades of meaning that contribute to the overall understanding of a passage.

Commentaries play a pivotal role in Fundamentalist scriptural study as well. While these commentaries vary in theological orientation, they offer insights into the historical, cultural, and theological dimensions of biblical texts. Fundamentalists often refer to works like "Matthew Henry's Commentary on the Whole Bible"[xv] or "The New American Commentary"[xvi] series to gain deeper insights into the meanings and implications of passages. These commentaries guide Fundamentalists through various interpretative lenses, helping them to discern the original intentions of the authors and the significance of the passages within the broader context of the Bible.

Fundamentalists employ a range of specialized tools and resources to undertake rigorous scriptural study. These tools, such as interlinear Bibles, concordances, lexicons, and commentaries, allow Fundamentalist scholars and practitioners to delve into the depths of the text, extract linguistic nuances, and uncover the historical and theological dimensions of the Scriptures. Through these resources, Fundamentalists seek to uphold their unwavering commitment to the core teachings of their faith and to gain a comprehensive understanding of the foundational texts that shape their beliefs.

3.4 Catholic Approach

3.4.1 Approaching the Word of God

Approaching Scripture from a theological perspective requires a combination of scholarly rigor, reverence, and an open heart to receive the divine message. Theological interpretation seeks to delve into the deeper meanings of the text, recognizing its spiritual dimensions and its significance for understanding God's nature and the human experience.

Historical and Literary Context: Understanding the historical and literary context of a passage is foundational to theological interpretation. For instance, in the Parable of the Prodigal Son (Luke 15:11-32), grasping the socio-cultural dynamics of the time and the intended audience helps unveil the depth of God's mercy and the profound reconciliation portrayed in the story. Contextual analysis prevents misinterpretation and fosters a more accurate theological understanding.

Theological Themes and Concepts: Scripture contains recurring themes and theological concepts that provide insights into God's character and plan for humanity. The concept of covenant, exemplified by God's covenant with Abraham (Genesis 15:1-6), carries theological significance throughout the Bible. The theological implications of covenant—faithfulness, promise, and relationship—can be traced across various passages, fostering a comprehensive understanding of God's interaction with His creation.

Christological Interpretation: A theological approach to Scripture often involves recognizing Christological implications in both the Old and New Testaments. For instance, Isaiah's prophecy of the "Suffering Servant" (Isaiah 53) is understood as a foreshadowing of Christ's redemptive sacrifice. By connecting

Old Testament prophecies to their fulfillment in Jesus, theological interpretation highlights the unity and purpose of God's plan of salvation.

Ethical and Moral Implications: Scripture provides moral and ethical guidance that informs Christian living. The Sermon on the Mount (Matthew 5-7) contains teachings on humility, forgiveness, and love for enemies. A theological perspective calls for not only understanding these teachings but also applying them to contemporary ethical challenges, fostering a transformative impact on believers' lives.

Theological Reflection and Dialogue: Engaging in theological reflection and dialogue helps individuals deepen their understanding of Scripture. For example, the dialogue between Jesus and Nicodemus (John 3:1-21) invites theological reflection on topics like rebirth, salvation, and the nature of faith. This dialogue serves as a model for believers to engage in conversations that lead to theological growth and exploration.

Prayerful Contemplation: A theological approach to Scripture goes beyond intellectual analysis; it involves prayerful contemplation to seek spiritual insights. The psalms, such as Psalm 23, invite believers to meditate on God's presence as a shepherd guiding and comforting His people. By engaging in contemplative practices, individuals can encounter God's truth and presence in a transformative manner.

Approaching Scripture from a theological perspective requires a multifaceted approach that encompasses historical context, theological themes, Christological connections, ethical implications, reflection, and contemplation. By embracing these dimensions, individuals can uncover the profound theological truths embedded within the pages of Scripture and deepen their understanding of God's nature and the Christian faith.

3.4.2 Difference between Exegesis and Eisegesis

Exegesis[xvii] and eisegesis[xviii] are two distinct approaches to interpreting religious texts, particularly the Bible, with significant implications for theological understanding. Exegesis involves a careful and objective analysis of the text to draw out its intended meaning within its historical, cultural, and literary context. Eisegesis, in contrast, the method often used by Fundamentalists and Creationists, involves reading personal or preconceived beliefs into the text, resulting in interpretations that may not align with the original intent of the text. Understanding these approaches is essential for maintaining the integrity of theological interpretation.

Exegesis, the preferred approach in sound theological scholarship, seeks to uncover the meaning of a text based on its original context and the author's intent. For example, in interpreting the parable of the Good Samaritan (Luke 10:25-37), exegesis would involve examining the socio-cultural dynamics of Samaritans and Jews during the time of Jesus, as well as understanding the intended moral lesson about compassion and neighborly love. By contextualizing the parable, exegesis helps to illuminate the original intention of the text and its implications for Christian living.

Eisegesis, on the other hand, can lead to distortions and misinterpretations by superimposing one's personal beliefs onto the text. An instance of eisegesis can be found in misinterpreting Psalm 23:1, "The Lord is my shepherd; I shall not want." Someone practicing eisegesis might focus solely on material prosperity and interpret "not wanting" as a promise of material wealth. However, exegesis reveals that the verse primarily conveys God's provision and care, which extends beyond material needs to spiritual well-being.

Another example involves the interpretation of Revelation 20:1-6, which discusses the concept of the millennium. Exegesis entails studying the various theological viewpoints and understanding the symbolism and literary style of the book of Revelation. In contrast, eisegesis could lead to dogmatic interpretations that promote specific end-time scenarios without a balanced consideration of the broader context of the book and the various ways the passage can be understood within the scope of Christian eschatology.

The distinction between exegesis and eisegesis is vital in theological interpretation. Exegesis aims to uncover the intended meaning of a text within its context, promoting accurate theological understanding. Eisegesis, on the other hand, can lead to distorted interpretations that reflect personal biases rather than the original message of the text. By utilizing exegesis and being cautious of eisegesis, theologians can maintain the integrity of their interpretations and contribute to a more informed and nuanced theological discourse.

3.4.3 The Use of Hermeneutics

Hermeneutics[xix], the art, and science of interpretation, plays a pivotal role when approaching Scripture from a theological perspective. The complexity and depth of the biblical text necessitate thoughtful engagement to uncover its profound theological truths. Hermeneutics provides a structured framework for understanding the historical, cultural, and literary context of the text, enabling theological insights to emerge.

Cultural and Historical Context: Hermeneutics emphasizes the importance of understanding the cultural and historical backdrop in which a passage was written. For instance, comprehending the significance of the "eye for an eye" principle in Exodus 21:24 requires recognizing its context within an ancient legal code. Applying hermeneutical principles enables theologians to discern the progression of ethical principles from the Old Testament to the teachings of Jesus, such as turning the other cheek (Matthew 5:38-39), reflecting a nuanced theological development.

Literary Genres and Styles: Different literary genres in the Bible demand distinct interpretive approaches. Hermeneutics helps differentiate between historical narratives, poetic imagery, parables, and prophetic utterances. The Song of Solomon, a poetic expression of love, contrasts with the historical account of the Exodus, highlighting the necessity of recognizing literary genres to draw out theological themes within each context.

Authorial Intent and Theological Themes: Hermeneutics underscores the significance of discerning the author's intended message while uncovering theological themes. Paul's epistles, such as Romans, contain intricate theological arguments that require careful analysis to grasp his intended teachings on justification, grace, and faith. Through hermeneutics, the theological richness of Paul's writings becomes accessible, contributing to a deeper understanding of Christian doctrine.

Christological Interpretation: Hermeneutics aids in recognizing Christological implications throughout Scripture. The Passover narrative in Exodus 12, with the blood of the lamb protecting Israel from the Angel of Death, foreshadows Christ's sacrificial role as the Lamb of God (John 1:29). Hermeneutics facilitates the identification of typological relationships, revealing the seamless continuity of Christ's redemptive mission within the Bible's diverse narratives.

Application to Contemporary Contexts: Hermeneutics bridges the temporal gap between the biblical world and the present, enabling the application of scriptural principles to contemporary contexts. The Parable of the Good Samaritan (Luke 10:25-37) inspires theological reflections on compassion and neighborly love, with implications for addressing social injustices today. Through hermeneutical engagement, theological principles are translated into actionable insights that resonate with current challenges.

Hermeneutics is indispensable when approaching Scripture from a theological perspective. It facilitates an informed understanding of cultural and historical contexts, recognizes diverse literary genres, unveils authorial intent, identifies Christological connections, and guides the application of theological principles to modern circumstances. By applying hermeneutical principles, theologians, and believers can navigate the complexities of the biblical text, extracting its profound theological insights for spiritual growth and faithful living.

3.4.4 Gaining a deeper understanding

Several other disciplines share similarities with hermeneutics in terms of interpretation, analysis, and understanding. Some of those disciplines include:

Semiotics: Semiotics[xx] is the study of signs and symbols, how they're used, and the meaning they convey. It also examines how these signs contribute to the creation of meaning in various contexts, similar to how hermeneutics explores textual meaning.

Literary Criticism: Literary criticism[xxi] involves analyzing and interpreting literary texts to uncover their layers of meaning, cultural contexts, and symbolism. Like hermeneutics, it delves into the interpretation of written works to understand their significance.

Cultural Studies: Cultural studies examine how culture shapes and is shaped by society. This interdisciplinary field analyzes various cultural artifacts, practices, and texts to understand their meanings and broader social implications, similar to hermeneutics' exploration of meanings within texts.

Philosophy of Language: This field delves into the nature of language, its relation to thought, and how it functions in communication. It shares similarities with hermeneutics in its exploration of how language conveys meaning and influences understanding.

Anthropology: Anthropology involves studying human cultures, societies, and behaviors. Ethnographic research often involves interpreting cultural practices, rituals, and narratives, akin to the interpretive work done in hermeneutics

Art History: Art historians interpret visual artworks to understand their cultural, historical, and aesthetic significance. Similar to hermeneutics, they analyze symbols, context, and intentions to decipher the meaning behind artworks.

Psychology of Perception: This field explores how humans perceive and interpret sensory information, including visual and auditory stimuli. It shares a connection with hermeneutics in terms of understanding how individuals construct meaning from sensory inputs.

Legal Interpretation: Legal scholars interpret laws, statutes, and legal texts to determine their meanings and implications. This practice involves similar skills to hermeneutics, as both disciplines involve careful textual analysis and interpretation.

Comparative Religion: Comparative religion involves studying various religious traditions and their texts to understand similarities, differences, and the meanings embedded within them. This parallels hermeneutics' exploration of religious texts and their interpretations.

Historical Analysis: Historians interpret historical documents, artifacts, and events to reconstruct the past and understand the broader historical context. This process shares common ground with hermeneutics in terms of analyzing texts within their temporal and cultural contexts.

These disciplines often involve the art of interpretation, seeking to understand the meaning, context, and significance of various forms of human expression. While they may differ in focus and approach, they all share the common thread of deciphering meanings from complex sources.

3.4.5 Is Sola Scriptura contained in the Bible?

The concept of Sola Scriptura[xxii], which upholds the Bible as the sole and ultimate authority in matters of faith and practice, is a central tenet of Protestant theology. However, from a Catholic perspective, while the Bible is certainly regarded as a vital and authoritative source of Christian doctrine, it is not the exclusive foundation upon which the entire faith is built. Instead, Catholic theology emphasizes a more comprehensive understanding that incorporates Scripture, Tradition, and the Magisterium (the teaching authority of the Church).

Catholics contend that the Bible itself does not explicitly advocate for the doctrine of Sola Scriptura. The Bible contains several passages that suggest the importance of Tradition and Apostolic authority alongside Scripture. In 2 Thessalonians 2:15, the apostle Paul instructs the Thessalonians to hold fast to both his teachings (oral tradition) and his written letters, indicating the coexistence of these two forms of transmission. Similarly, 1

Timothy 3:15 refers to the Church as the "pillar and foundation of the truth," underlining the role of the Church as a living authority that plays a pivotal role in safeguarding and interpreting the Christian faith.

The Catholic perspective recognizes the Bible as an indispensable part of the deposit of faith, but it maintains that Tradition and the Magisterium are equally essential. The Second Vatican Council's "Dei Verbum"[xxiii] document (Dogmatic Constitution on Divine Revelation) explicitly affirms the unity of Scripture and Tradition, asserting that both sources flow from the same divine wellspring. This understanding acknowledges the ongoing role of the Holy Spirit in guiding the Church's interpretation of Scripture and Tradition.

The Catholic perspective on Sola Scriptura emphasizes the interplay between Scripture, Tradition, and the Magisterium in shaping the Christian faith. While the Bible holds a central place in Catholic theology, it is not viewed in isolation but rather in conjunction with the living Tradition of the Church and the guidance of the Magisterium. The passages in Scripture that address the importance of Apostolic teaching and Church authority further reinforce this holistic approach to understanding the foundations of the faith.

4 Theological   perspectives   of Genesis

Genesis, as the foundational book of the Bible, holds a pivotal position in religious traditions worldwide due to its transcendent theological significance.

Understanding the historical context of Genesis within the ancient Near Eastern world provides valuable insights into the cultural influences and theological polemics embedded in the text. Comparative studies have highlighted parallels and distinctions with other creation myths and religious traditions, further elucidating the unique contributions and perspectives of Genesis.

Analyzing the literary structure of Genesis uncovers a thematic emphasis on creation, covenant, sin, redemption, and the formation of Israel as God's chosen people. Genesis presents not one, but two distinct creation narratives (Genesis 1 and 2), each offering theological insights about God's sovereignty, creativity, and purpose in fashioning the cosmos. The concept of humanity being created in the "Image of God" raises profound theological questions about human dignity, responsibility, and our relationship with the Creator. This notion has significant implications for how humans understand their purpose and how they should relate to one another and the world around them.

Moreover, Genesis presents humanity as stewards of God's creation, entrusted with the care and preservation of the natural world. This theological perspective emphasizes the importance of responsible ecological practices, making Genesis relevant to contemporary discussions on environmental ethics and sustainability.

The Fall narrative in Genesis 3 delves into the theological implications of human disobedience and sin, leading to estrangement from God and a broken relationship with creation. This narrative highlights the complexities of human nature and the consequences of moral choices, resonating with ethical and philosophical discussions on human responsibility and free will.

Genesis further establishes the foundation for God's redemptive plan by introducing God's covenant with Abraham in Genesis 12. This covenant forms the basis for God's promises to bless and redeem humanity through a chosen people. The giving of the Law to Moses in the book of Exodus and the establishment of the Mosaic covenant reflect God's desire for a holy and just society, revealing divine expectations for human conduct and communal life.

The stories of Abraham, Isaac, Jacob, and Joseph in Genesis exemplify the significance of faith, obedience, and divine providence in the unfolding of God's redemptive plan. These narratives illustrate the complexities of human relationships and the transformative power of divine grace, offering timeless lessons on forgiveness, reconciliation, and the path to redemption.

Theological perspectives on Genesis enrich our understanding of the text's spiritual significance, presenting a multi-layered interpretation that transcends time and cultural boundaries. By delving into its historical context, employing diverse interpretation methods, and exploring its thematic richness, we gain profound theological insights into the Genesis narratives. As we continue to explore this foundational text, we deepen our appreciation for its enduring relevance in shaping religious beliefs, ethical principles, and the eternal quest for meaning and purpose in human existence.

Genesis stands as a timeless and invaluable text, offering profound theological insights into the nature of God, humanity, creation, and the divine-human relationship. Its exploration through historical and literary analysis, alongside diverse theological perspectives, provides a comprehensive understanding of the text's enduring significance in shaping human understanding and spiritual life. The profound lessons within the Genesis narratives continue to resonate with individuals and communities worldwide, guiding their moral and spiritual journeys throughout history and into the future.

4.1 Genesis as Ancient Literature

The book of Genesis, the first book of the Hebrew Bible and the Christian Old Testament, holds a central place in the religious and cultural heritage of Judaism and Christianity. It recounts the origins of the world, humanity, and the chosen people of Israel. For centuries, scholars have studied Genesis as a unique piece of ancient literature, seeking to understand its literary genre, historical context, and theological implications. While exploring the characteristics of Genesis as ancient literature, we draw on textual evidence and Scriptural references to shed light on its profound significance.

Genesis is a remarkable example of ancient Hebrew narrative literature. It employs a distinctive style characterized by vivid storytelling, genealogies, and poetic elements. The author skillfully weaves together various narrative threads to form a cohesive and captivating narrative. The first few chapters, particularly the Creation account in Genesis 1-2, display a poetic structure, evoking imagery and symbolism (Genesis 1:1-31; 2:1-3). In contrast, the following chapters adopt a more straightforward narrative style, chronicling the lives of the patriarchs and matriarchs with rich detail and dialogue (Genesis

12:1-9; 18:1-15). The use of parallelism and repetition in certain passages (Genesis 6:5-8; 7:1-5) further highlights the literary artistry of Genesis.

Genesis emerges from a remote historical setting, deeply rooted in ancient Near Eastern culture and traditions. Scholars recognize that the text incorporates motifs and themes that were prevalent in ancient Mesopotamian and Egyptian societies. The account of the Great Flood, for instance, shares striking similarities with the flood narratives from the Epic of Gilgamesh and the Atrahasis epic. Nevertheless, Genesis distinguishes itself by presenting a monotheistic worldview, where the God of Israel is the sole Creator and Sovereign over the entire cosmos (Genesis 1:1; 14:22). The text also offers valuable insights into the social structures, customs, and religious practices of its time, contributing to our understanding of ancient civilizations.

Beyond its historical and literary aspects, Genesis carries profound theological implications. The opening chapters establish the foundation of Judeo-Christian theology by affirming the divine origin of the universe and humanity's unique status as bearers of the divine image (Genesis 1:27). The Fall of humanity into sin and the subsequent promise of redemption through a chosen seed (Genesis 3:15) lay the groundwork for the entire biblical narrative. God's covenantal relationship with figures like Abraham (Genesis 12:1-3), Isaac (Genesis 26:2-5), and Jacob (Genesis 28:10-15) are pivotal in shaping Israel's identity as a chosen nation with a divine purpose.

Genesis stands as a literary masterpiece and a theological cornerstone of ancient literature. Its narrative artistry, historical context, and theological significance continue to captivate scholars and believers alike. As we delve into the pages of Genesis, we encounter a profound portrayal of humanity's relationship with its Creator, the complexities of divine providence, and the enduring themes of faith, obedience, and covenantal promise. Through this ancient text, we gain a deeper understanding of the origins of faith and the enduring relevance of its message across cultures and generations.

4.2 Theological Themes in Genesis

The book of Genesis serves as a theological treasure trove, presenting foundational themes that lay the groundwork for the rest of the biblical narrative. There are important theological riches found within Genesis that shape the understanding of God, humanity, sin, redemption, and covenant in both Jewish and Christian traditions. Drawing upon Scriptural references, we unveil the profound theological insights embedded within this ancient and sacred text.

Genesis commences with the majestic account of God's creative act, where He fashions the heavens, the earth, and all living beings out of nothingness (Genesis 1:1-31). This narrative emphasizes God's sovereignty as the Supreme Creator and underscores the goodness of His creation. The refrain "And God saw that it was good" echoes throughout the Creation story, signifying the divine intention for a harmonious and ordered cosmos. The theological foundation of God as the sole source of all existence permeates the entirety of Genesis, underpinning subsequent narratives.

Despite the harmonious beginning, Genesis portrays humanity's tragic choice to rebel against God's command, leading to the Fall and the entry of sin into the world (Genesis 3:1-24). This event profoundly shapes the biblical understanding of human nature, revealing the inherent inclination toward disobedience and sin. The consequences of Adam and Eve's disobedience extend to all generations, leaving humanity separated from God. This theological theme of human sinfulness lays the groundwork for the need for redemption and restoration throughout the biblical narrative.

Genesis introduces the concept of divine promise and covenant as essential theological themes. God's covenantal faithfulness is demonstrated through His interactions with individuals like Noah (Genesis 6:18), Abraham (Genesis 15:18), and Jacob (Genesis 28:13-15). The Abrahamic Covenant, in particular, stands as a pivotal promise in Genesis, highlighting God's commitment to bless all nations through Abraham's descendants (Genesis 12:2-3). This covenantal promise becomes the foundation for the formation of the people of Israel and foreshadows the ultimate fulfillment of God's redemptive plan in Jesus Christ.

Genesis provides numerous examples of faith and obedience as essential elements of a righteous relationship with God. Abraham, often referred to as the father of faith, exhibits unwavering trust in God's promises, even in the face of uncertainty (Genesis 12:4; 22:1-18). Similarly, Joseph exemplifies obedience and faithfulness amidst challenging circumstances, leading to the preservation of his family and the fulfillment of God's plan (Genesis 39:1-6; 45:4-8). These examples highlight the theological significance of faith and obedience as integral components of a covenantal relationship with God.

Genesis serves as a theological tapestry, woven with profound insights into God's nature, humanity's condition, and the unfolding drama of redemption. The theological themes of Creation, the Fall, divine promise, and covenantal faithfulness reverberate throughout the biblical narrative, culminating in the person and work of Jesus Christ. As believers engage with the theological depth of Genesis, they discover timeless truths that continue to shape their understanding of God's character, His plan of redemption, and the call to faithful obedience. This ancient text continues to inspire and guide individuals and communities in their journey of faith and discipleship.

4.3 Historical and Literary Context of Genesis

Understanding the historical and literary context of the book of Genesis is essential for interpreting its narratives, themes, and theological messages accurately. Examination of the ancient world in which Genesis was composed is essential, exploring the historical background and literary features that shaped the text. By examining the cultural milieu and literary conventions of its time, we can gain deeper insights into the significance of Genesis within its historical context.

The historical context of Genesis is closely tied to the ancient Near Eastern civilizations, particularly Mesopotamia. Comparative studies reveal striking similarities and differences between Genesis and Mesopotamian creation myths, such as Enuma Elish, shedding light on the unique theological contributions of Genesis.

Understanding the religious beliefs and practices of ancient Near Eastern societies helps us appreciate the theological polemics and distinctiveness of Genesis in portraying monotheism, creation ex nihilo, and the concept of a personal, covenantal God.

Genesis is part of the Pentateuch, comprising the first five books of the Bible. Examining the literary structure and coherence of the Pentateuch elucidates the interconnectedness of its narratives and theological themes.

Genealogies in Genesis serve multiple purposes, including tracing lineage, establishing historical connections, and conveying theological messages about divine promises and covenants.

Genesis employs narrative prose and poetic forms, each serving specific literary and theological functions. Identifying these literary elements enhances our understanding of the text's intended meaning.

The Documentary Hypothesis[xxiv] proposes that the Pentateuch, including Genesis, is a composite work of multiple sources (J, E, D, P). Exploring the origins of this theory and its impact on the understanding of Genesis is crucial for comprehending its historical context.

Scholars have identified distinctive styles, vocabulary, and theological emphases within Genesis, attributing them to different sources. Understanding these sources enriches our appreciation of the text's diverse literary layers.

Genesis covers the lives of the patriarchs - Abraham, Isaac, Jacob, and Joseph. Exploring the historical setting and themes of this period reveals the theological significance of God's covenantal promises and the formation of Israel as a chosen people.

Examining ancient cultural practices, customs, and social norms during the patriarchal period illuminates the context in which the narratives unfold.

The Flood narrative in Genesis shares similarities with other flood stories from various ancient cultures. Exploring these parallels helps to discern the unique theological message conveyed in Genesis.

Understanding the theological themes of divine judgment, preservation of life, and covenantal promises within the Flood narrative enriches our comprehension of God's relationship with humanity.

The historical and literary context of Genesis provides a valuable backdrop for interpreting its narratives and theological teachings. By exploring the cultural, religious, and literary milieu of the ancient Near East, we gain a deeper appreciation for the distinctive contributions of Genesis to religious thought and the development of monotheistic theology. Understanding the context in which Genesis was composed enhances our ability to grasp its enduring significance and relevance as a foundational text for multiple religious traditions.

4.4 Theological significance of Genesis as the foundational book

Genesis holds a unique position as the opening book of the Bible, setting the stage for the entire biblical narrative. Its theological significance as the foundational book extends across religious traditions, shaping core beliefs about God, creation, humanity, and the divine-human relationship. There are profound theological teachings found within Genesis and its lasting impact on religious thought and practice.

Genesis introduces God as the sovereign Creator of the universe, fashioning all things ex nihilo (out of nothing). This foundational concept shapes the understanding of God's omnipotence and the nature of the world as a purposeful creation.

The portrayal of God in Genesis as a personal and covenantal deity establishes the foundation for a relational and intimate bond between God and humanity.

The Abrahamic and Mosaic covenants reveal God's faithfulness to His promises, illustrating His enduring commitment to humanity despite human failings.

The theological concept of humanity created in the "Image of God" imparts inherent dignity, value, and purpose to all human beings, regardless of race, ethnicity, or social status.

The Fall narrative highlights the human capacity for both moral choice and disobedience. Genesis exposes the brokenness of the human condition while underscoring the need for redemption and restoration.

The stories of forgiveness and redemption, exemplified in the lives of Abraham, Joseph, and others, underscore God's gracious offer of reconciliation to humanity.

God's covenant with Abraham and his descendants serves as a theological foundation for God's chosen people, Israel. The promises of land, descendants, and blessing convey God's redemptive plan for all nations.

The covenant established with Moses on Mount Sinai presents the principles of justice, holiness, and ethical conduct, forming the basis for Israel's religious and moral life.

The narratives in Genesis depict God's providential care, orchestrating events for the fulfillment of His purposes in the lives of individuals and nations.

Instances of divine guidance, such as Joseph's rise to power in Egypt or Jacob's wrestling with God, reveal God's involvement in human affairs and His willingness to interact with humanity.

The theological themes of creation and redemption are intricately woven together in Genesis, emphasizing God's continuous work of bringing order out of chaos and redeeming humanity from sin.

Genesis foreshadows the ultimate redemptive plan of God through the Messianic promise (Genesis 3:15), prefiguring the role of Jesus Christ as the Savior of the world.

The theological significance of Genesis as the foundational book of the Bible lies in its profound teachings about God, humanity, creation, and the divine-human relationship. As the initial installment of the biblical narrative, Genesis establishes the theological framework that shapes religious thought, ethical principles, and the understanding of human existence for diverse religious traditions. The theological themes of creation, covenant, sin, and redemption intertwine to create a cohesive narrative of God's purposeful and redemptive engagement with humanity. As readers engage with Genesis, they encounter a theological tapestry that spans generations, providing timeless lessons on faith, obedience, grace, and the divine plan for reconciliation.

4.5 Interpretation methods and approaches to Genesis

The interpretation of Genesis has been a subject of scholarly inquiry and theological reflection for centuries. As the foundational book of the Bible, Genesis contains diverse narratives, theological themes, and literary styles. There are various interpretation methods and approaches applied to Genesis, ranging from historical-critical analysis to theological hermeneutics. By understanding these approaches, readers can navigate the complexities of Genesis and derive deeper insights from its profound teachings.

Historical-critical analysis examines the historical setting, cultural background, and authorship of Genesis. Scholars draw upon archaeological, linguistic, and historical data to contextualize the text within its ancient Near Eastern environment.

Scholars applying source criticism identify distinct sources (J, E, D, P) within Genesis, exploring how these sources may have been combined and redacted over time.

Form criticism analyzes the literary forms and genres present in Genesis, distinguishing between myths, genealogies, narratives, and poetry. This approach sheds light on the diverse functions and purposes of each literary form.

Literary scholars analyze the structure of Genesis to discern patterns, repetitions, and thematic development throughout the book. Identifying chiastic structures and narrative cycles enhances the understanding of theological messages.

Focusing on narrative elements, this approach examines character development, plot dynamics, and rhetorical devices to uncover the intended meaning and theological significance of the stories.

The poetic sections in Genesis (e.g., the Song of Lamech, Genesis 4:23-24) offer unique theological insights. Poetic analysis explores the use of parallelism, metaphors, and imagery to grasp the underlying theological themes.

Theological hermeneutics considers Genesis within the broader context of the entire Bible. This approach recognizes the interconnectedness of biblical texts, allowing themes and concepts from other parts of Scripture to inform the interpretation of Genesis.

Theological hermeneutics also seeks Christological insights in Genesis, viewing the narratives and characters as foreshadowing or types pointing to the person and work of Jesus Christ.

Some theologians have employed allegorical interpretations of Genesis, seeing the narratives as symbolic representations of deeper spiritual truths. This approach may draw parallels between events in Genesis and Christian teachings.

Typological interpretation looks for foreshadowings or "types" of Christ or other biblical figures in the characters or events of Genesis.

Interpreting Genesis involves drawing ethical and moral lessons from narratives, offering guidance for contemporary living and ethical decision-making.

Applying the timeless theological teachings of Genesis to modern contexts fosters relevance and practical application in the lives of believers.

Interpreting Genesis requires a multifaceted approach that integrates historical-critical analysis, literary methods, theological hermeneutics, and figurative interpretation. By engaging with diverse approaches, readers can explore the depth and richness of Genesis' theological themes, discovering its enduring significance for faith, ethics, and understanding of God's redemptive plan. As we navigate the interpretative complexities, the theological treasures of Genesis unveil themselves, inspiring spiritual growth, and fostering a deeper appreciation for the sacred text.

4.6 Theological implications of creation narratives

The creation narratives in Genesis (Genesis 1:1 - 2:3 and Genesis 2:4-25) hold a central place in the Bible and are foundational to various religious traditions. These narratives offer profound theological insights into the nature of God, the purpose of creation, and humanity's role within it. It is necessary to explore the creation narratives, examining their literary structure, theological themes, and implications for understanding the relationship between God, humanity, and the natural world.

Genesis 1:1 - 2:3: The first creation narrative portrays God's orderly and purposeful act of creation over six days, culminating in the Sabbath's rest. The structure of "days" highlights the divine intentionality in bringing order to the cosmos. Genesis 2:4-25: The second creation narrative provides a more intimate and focused account of the creation of humanity, emphasizing the relationship between Adam, Eve, and God. This narrative complements the broader scope of Genesis 1, offering a more personalized perspective.

Both narratives emphasize God's role as the supreme Creator of the universe. The term "Elohim" in Genesis 1 denotes God's power and transcendence, while "Yahweh Elohim" in Genesis 2 reflects His personal and covenantal nature.

The creation narratives affirm that God created the world "out of nothing" (ex nihilo). This theological concept underscores God's absolute authority over creation and distinguishes Him from other ancient Near Eastern creation myths[xxv].

The meticulous sequence of creation in Genesis 1 underscores God's intentionality and purpose in forming the cosmos and all living beings. This orderliness reflects God's wisdom and sovereignty.

The creation narratives portray humanity as God's appointed stewards of the earth. The divine mandate to "fill the earth and subdue it" (Genesis 1:28) implies a responsibility to care for and cultivate God's creation.

The creation narratives call for awe and reverence toward the natural world as a reflection of God's creativity and glory. This theological perspective fosters environmental stewardship and care for the earth.

The concept of humanity created in the "Image of God" (Genesis 1:26-27) imbues every individual with inherent dignity and value. This theological teaching has implications for ethics, social justice, and the treatment of others.

Understanding the creation narratives as theological affirmations rather than scientific accounts allows for greater harmony between faith and scientific discoveries about the natural world.

The creation narratives have been interpreted both literally and figuratively. Theological considerations and scientific discoveries have prompted diverse perspectives on the nature of the creation accounts.

Applying historical-critical methods to the creation of narratives raises questions about their literary sources and intended messages.

The creation narratives were written in the ancient cosmological context, raising questions about their compatibility with modern scientific understandings of the universe's origins.

The creation narratives in Genesis offer theological insights that resonate across religious traditions and human cultures. Understanding these narratives as theological affirmations of God's creative power, purpose, and humanity's role within creation fosters a deeper appreciation for the divine order in the cosmos. As readers engage with the creation narratives, they encounter profound truths about God's sovereignty, humanity's stewardship, and the inherent dignity of every individual. The theological implications of these narratives extend beyond the pages of Genesis, inspiring ethical conduct, environmental responsibility, and a deeper reverence for the Creator and His creation.

4.7 Examining the role of human beings in the created order

The creation narratives in Genesis establish the unique position of human beings in the created order. As the crown of God's creation, humanity holds a significant role and responsibility within the natural world. It is necessary to explore the theological understanding of humanity's role as portrayed in Genesis and its implications for ethical conduct, stewardship, and the divine-human relationship.

The concept of humanity created in the "Image of God" (Genesis 1:26-27) conveys the inherent dignity and value of every individual. This theological teaching underscores the unique status of human beings among all living creatures.

Recognizing the Image of God in every person calls for ethical treatment, respect for human life, and the promotion of human rights and dignity.

Genesis 1:28 bestows upon humanity the divine mandate to "fill the earth and subdue it." This responsibility portrays human beings as stewards of God's creation, entrusted with its care and preservation.

The role of stewards necessitates ethical practices in resource management, environmental conservation, and sustainable development.

God's command to humanity to have dominion over the earth is not an authorization for exploitation but a call to responsibly manage and protect the natural world.

Understanding human beings' interconnectedness with the rest of creation fosters ecological consciousness and a sense of responsibility for the well-being of all living creatures.

The Fall narrative (Genesis 3) portrays the rupture in the divine-human relationship due to sin. The consequences of the Fall affect humanity's relationship with God, fellow humans, and the environment.

The Fall underscores the need for redemption and restoration, highlighting the brokenness of the world and the human condition.

The biblical narrative unfolds as God initiates a redemptive plan to reconcile humanity and creation to Himself. This plan culminates in the person and work of Jesus Christ.

Through Christ, the divine-human relationship is restored, calling humanity to embody God's love, compassion, and justice in the world.

Understanding humanity's role in the created order motivates social responsibility and advocacy for justice, equality, and compassion toward all people.

The recognition of human stewardship encourages responsible ecological practices, promoting sustainability and care for the environment.

Understanding humanity's role in the created order raises questions about life's purpose and the pursuit of meaning beyond material achievements.

Recognizing the divine call to be bearers of God's image inspires individuals to seek deeper spiritual connections and align their lives with God's purposes.

Examining the role of human beings in the created order reveals the theological significance of humanity as God's Image-bearers and stewards of His creation. The recognition of human dignity and responsibility calls for ethical conduct, environmental stewardship, and compassionate social engagement. Understanding humanity's place in the divine plan fosters a deeper sense of purpose, aligning human actions with God's redemptive purposes in the world. As we reflect on humanity's role in the created order, we are invited to embrace our unique calling as partners with God in caring for His world and embodying His love, justice, and compassion toward all creation.

5 Authorship

5.1 Authorship and Historical Context of Genesis

The book of Genesis, as the opening chapter of the Hebrew Bible and Christian Old Testament, holds significant historical and theological importance. There are intriguing questions surrounding the authorship and historical context of Genesis. Exploring the textual evidence and relevant Scriptural references, we aim to shed light on the origins and background of this ancient and sacred book.

The authorship of Genesis has been a subject of scholarly debate for centuries. Traditionally, both Jewish and Christian traditions ascribe the book's authorship to Moses, a central figure in Israel's history and the receiver of the Law (Exodus 17:14; Numbers 33:1-2). This belief is based partly on the presence of Mosaic elements in the narrative, such as laws and genealogies. Additionally, Jesus Himself attributed certain portions of the Pentateuch, including Genesis, to Moses (Mark 10:3-5; Luke 24:27). However, modern scholarship has put forward the Documentary Hypothesis, suggesting that multiple sources contributed to the composition of Genesis, with the final editing likely occurring during or after the Babylonian exile.

The historical context of Genesis spans a vast timeframe, encompassing events from the creation of the world to the time of the patriarchs. The first eleven chapters narrate primeval history, including the creation account, the Fall, the flood narrative, and the dispersion of languages at Babel. These accounts share similarities with other ancient Near Eastern texts, reflecting the cultural milieu of the region during the second and first millennia BCE. The latter part of Genesis, from chapter 12 onwards, shifts its focus to the lives of the patriarchs, such as Abraham, Isaac, Jacob, and Joseph. These narratives are set in a historical context that predates the conquest of Canaan and portrays the formative years of the Israelite nation.

The historical accuracy of Genesis has been a point of contention. While some view the narratives as historically reliable, others interpret them as theological accounts that convey spiritual truths rather than precise historical events. The creation account, for instance, presents theological themes such as God's sovereignty, the goodness of creation, and humanity's unique relationship with the Creator, while not conforming to scientific explanations. Similarly, the accounts of the patriarchs highlight themes of faith, obedience, and divine promise, emphasizing God's faithfulness to His covenant.

The historical context of Genesis suggests that the stories contained within it were likely transmitted orally through generations before being committed to writing. Ancient cultures often relied on oral traditions to pass down sacred stories and historical accounts. Over time, these oral traditions were compiled and edited into written form, possibly during the time of Moses or later during the Babylonian exile when there was a renewed interest in preserving Israel's history and identity.

The authorship and historical context of Genesis remain complex and multifaceted topics that have intrigued scholars and believers for generations. The traditional attribution of authorship to Moses aligns with long-held beliefs, while the Documentary Hypothesis offers an alternative perspective based on textual analysis. Regardless of its origins, Genesis holds invaluable historical and theological insights that shape the foundations of Judaism and Christianity. As readers engage with the text, they encounter timeless truths about God's creative power, humanity's condition, and the unfolding plan of redemption. Understanding the authorship and historical background enhances our appreciation of Genesis as an ancient and sacred book that continues to inspire and guide individuals and communities on their spiritual journey.

5.2 Fundamentalist View

The question of authorship and the historical origins of the Pentateuch, the first five books of the Old Testament, has been a subject of considerable scholarly debate. One prominent view among conservative religious circles is the Fundamentalist perspective, which upholds the belief in Mosaic authorship.

There are several arguments in support of this view. A few of them are:

Fundamentalists argue that the Pentateuch represents the direct revelation of God to Moses. As such, it possesses divine authority and authenticity, necessitating Mosaic authorship to preserve the veracity of the text.

Moses, as the leader and lawgiver of the Israelites, had the unique role of recording the divine laws, covenants, and historical events, creating testamentary literature for the people of Israel. This role lends credibility to the belief that he authored the Pentateuch.

Fundamentalists point to various passages within the Pentateuch where Moses is explicitly identified as the writer (Exodus 17:14; Numbers 33:2; Deuteronomy 31:9). These textual references provide strong indications of Mosaic authorship.

Advocates of Mosaic authorship argue that the seamless narrative flow throughout the Pentateuch suggests a single author. The consistent use of certain terms, themes, and stylistic elements further supports this claim.

The detailed legal codes and governance principles presented in the Pentateuch align closely with Moses' role as a leader and lawgiver. This correspondence strengthens the case for Mosaic authorship.

Early Jewish tradition, as found in the Talmud[xxvi] and Mishnah[xxvii], affirms the belief in Mosaic authorship. Fundamentalists find support in these traditional Jewish interpretations of the Pentateuch.

The early Christian Church widely held the view of Mosaic authorship, as evidenced by the writings of influential Church Fathers such as Augustine[xxviii], Origen[xxix], and Jerome[xxx]. This historical witness adds weight to the Fundamentalist perspective.

The Mosaic authorship of the Pentateuch has faced criticism from modern higher-critical approaches, which propose multiple authorship and later redaction. Fundamentalists engage with these criticisms and offer counterarguments, emphasizing the historical reliability and divine inspiration of the biblical text.

The Fundamentalist view on Mosaic authorship for the Pentateuch rests upon theological, historical, and biblical foundations. By upholding the belief that Moses served as the primary author under divine inspiration, this perspective seeks to preserve the authoritative nature of the Scriptures and affirm the significance of Moses as a central figure in Israel's history and religious tradition. While acknowledging the complexities of the authorship debate, Fundamentalists remain steadfast in their commitment to the divine origin and authorship of the Pentateuch by Moses.

5.3 Documentary Hypothesis

The traditional belief among Fundamentalist Christians is that Moses was the sole author of the Pentateuch, the first five books of the Bible. While this perspective is deeply rooted in the Christian tradition and has its merits, it faces challenges when considering certain passages within the scriptures themselves. One such passage that merits examination is Deuteronomy 34:1-12, which narrates the death, mourning, and burial of Moses.

Considering the traditional belief in Mosaic authorship, this account poses an intriguing paradox. How could Moses have written about his death and burial if the Pentateuch indeed originated from his pen? This enigma opens the door to a more nuanced consideration of the composition of the Bible, recognizing that it is the result of a complex process involving multiple authors and editors over centuries. This perspective does not diminish the divine inspiration of scripture but rather underscores the human aspect of its composition.

The Fundamentalist view on Mosaic authorship for the Pentateuch rests upon theological, historical, and biblical foundations. By upholding the belief that Moses served as the primary author under divine inspiration, this perspective seeks to preserve the authoritative nature of the Scriptures and affirm the significance of Moses as a central figure in Israel's history and religious tradition. While acknowledging the complexities of the authorship debate, Fundamentalists remain steadfast in their commitment to the divine origin and authorship of the Pentateuch by Moses.

To present a balanced argument, it is essential to provide an overview of the JEDP view and the reasons that support its acceptance.

The Documentary Hypothesis, a form of Literary Criticism, is also known as the JEDP theory which presents a compelling and widely accepted approach to understanding the authorship of the Pentateuch. The hypothesis posits that the Pentateuch is not the work of a single author, such as Moses, but rather a composite of four distinct sources: the Yahwist (J), Elohist (E), Deuteronomist (D), and Priestly (P) sources. This theory is supported by a wealth of textual evidence, linguistic analysis, and historical context that highlight the diversity of styles, themes, and theological perspectives found within the Pentateuch.

One of the primary strengths of the Documentary Hypothesis is its ability to account for the repetitive and contradictory elements in the Pentateuch. Through careful analysis, scholars have identified instances where different sources offer varying accounts of the same events or laws, suggesting multiple authors at work. This critical examination of the text has yielded a more nuanced understanding of the complexities involved in its composition.

Linguistic analysis has also played a significant role in supporting the Documentary Hypothesis. Distinctive vocabulary, linguistic features, and variations in the use of divine names (Yahweh vs. Elohim) throughout the Pentateuch provide strong indicators of different sources. This linguistic evidence bolsters the idea of multiple authors, each with their distinct characteristics and contributions.

The diverse theological perspectives and thematic motifs found within the Pentateuch further support the Documentary Hypothesis. The J, E, D and P sources offer unique insights into the religious beliefs, practices, and narratives of different periods in ancient Israel's history. This diversity of theological thought aligns well with the idea of multiple authors writing from different contexts.

Archaeological discoveries and comparative studies with other ancient Near Eastern texts[xxxi] have provided additional evidence for the Documentary Hypothesis. Similarities in legal codes, ritual practices, and narrative structures between the Pentateuch and other ancient texts from the region suggest literary and cultural influences on the composition of the Pentateuch.

The Documentary Hypothesis also offers a coherent explanation for the various literary styles and genres present within the Pentateuch. The J source is characterized by its vivid and anthropomorphic portrayals of God and the use of stories to convey theological truths, while the P source focuses heavily on genealogies, rituals, and priestly concerns. This diversity of literary approaches is more easily explained by multiple authors than by a single writer like Moses.

The acceptance of the Documentary Hypothesis aligns with the historical development of biblical scholarship and the evolution of critical methods. Over the centuries, scholars have increasingly recognized the complexities of the Pentateuch and embraced the idea of multiple sources as the most plausible explanation.

The Documentary Hypothesis has gained widespread acceptance and support from numerous scholars across different theological and academic backgrounds. Its wide appeal and the recognition it has received in academic circles lend credibility to this approach.

While the Mosaic authorship view is rooted in traditional religious beliefs, the Documentary Hypothesis offers a more comprehensive and scholarly explanation for the Pentateuch's composition. It encourages an open-minded engagement with the text, promoting a deeper understanding of the Bible's historical and literary dimensions.

Embracing the Documentary Hypothesis does not diminish the spiritual or theological significance of the Pentateuch. Rather, it enriches our understanding of the text by acknowledging the complex process of its formation and the contributions of various ancient authors, redactors, and editors. By accepting the Documentary Hypothesis, we can engage with the Pentateuch from a more informed and intellectually rigorous perspective, deepening our appreciation for its profound impact on ancient Israelite society and the development of religious thought.

However, let us be clear that our exploration is not driven by an intent to cast doubt on the veracity of the Bible or to undermine its spiritual significance. On the contrary, our journey seeks to enrich our understanding of the Word of God and to reconcile it with the findings of modern science and historical research. The pursuit of knowledge should not be feared but embraced to strengthen our faith and deepen our appreciation for the divine mysteries.

6 Fundamentalist and Creationist View of Creation

6.1 Two tales of creation

Genesis, the first book of the Bible, lays the groundwork for the Judeo-Christian understanding of the origins of the universe, Earth, and humanity. Within its opening chapters, we encounter two distinct accounts of creation, often referred to as the "creation stories." Which account should be believed? These narratives have sparked numerous debates and discussions over the centuries, prompting theologians and scientists alike to grapple with the apparent contradictions they present.

The First Creation Account (Genesis 1):

The first creation account, found in Genesis chapter 1, outlines a majestic and systematic portrayal of the creative acts of God. In this account, God creates the world in six days, separating light from darkness, the waters above from the waters below, and bringing forth land, vegetation, celestial bodies, marine life, and terrestrial creatures. Finally, on the sixth day, God creates humanity, "male and female" in His image, entrusting them with stewardship over the earth.

This narrative is marked by its poetic structure and rhythm, emphasizing God's sovereignty and divine authority over creation. The use of numbered days and the repetitive phrase "God saw that it was good" underscores the ordered and purposeful nature of the creative process. The theological message conveyed here centers on God's benevolent act of bringing forth a harmonious and purposeful world.

The Second Creation Account (Genesis 2):

In contrast, the second creation account, found in Genesis chapter 2, provides a more intimate and personal depiction of creation. This narrative zooms in on the details of the formation of the first human, referred to as "man" (adam), fashioned from the dust of the ground. God breathes life into this earthly being, making him a "living soul." Subsequently, God creates a garden, places man in it, and forms animals from the ground as potential companions for him.

In this account, the focus shifts from the cosmic scale to the human level, emphasizing the special relationship between God and humanity. The intimate portrayal of God "walking in the garden" and conversing with Adam portrays a sense of closeness and involvement. The theological emphasis lies in humanity's unique position as stewards of the earth and the potential for a deep, personal relationship with the divine.

The apparent discrepancies between these two accounts have spurred much scholarly discussion. Some interpret these differing narratives as evidence of multiple sources woven together in the Pentateuch, each with distinct theological emphases and cultural contexts. This perspective, often referred to as the Documentary Hypothesis, posits that ancient editors or redactors compiled these accounts to preserve the spiritual truths held by various traditions.

Others seek to reconcile these narratives by exploring their symbolic and metaphorical dimensions. Rather than viewing them as scientific treatises or historical records, they emphasize the theological messages and moral teachings embedded within the text. This approach allows for a harmonious interpretation, recognizing the creative power of God expressed through diverse literary styles.

Moreover, approaching the creation accounts with a scientific lens invites us to explore the compatibility between the theological truths they convey and the insights of modern cosmology and evolutionary biology. Many scholars and theologians argue that biblical creation accounts are not meant to provide scientific explanations of the physical universe but rather to reveal God's sovereignty and the purposeful nature of existence.

Theological and scientific literacy equips us to explore the nuances of these accounts, understanding that the profundity of scripture lies not solely in the details but in the spiritual truths they impart. Embracing both the theological and scientific dimensions enriches our appreciation of the creative power of God and our place within the grand tapestry of existence. Together, let us seek to harmonize the wisdom of ancient scriptures with the discoveries of modern knowledge, drawing ever closer to the divine truth that unites both realms.

6.2 Age of the Earth

The age of the Earth has been a subject of significant debate and discussion within the realms of Creationism and Fundamentalism. While both perspectives are grounded in a shared belief in the divine origin of the universe, their approaches to determining the precise age of the Earth diverge due to their interpretations of Scripture and scientific evidence.

From the Creationist perspective, adherents generally advocate for a Young Earth, typically dating the Earth's age to around 6,000 to 10,000 years old. This dating aligns with a literal interpretation of the genealogies found in the Bible, particularly in the book of Genesis. By tracing the lineage from Adam to key figures in biblical history, Creationists calculate the age of the Earth based on these genealogical records. Notably, Bishop

James Ussher[xxxii], an influential 17th-century scholar, famously dated the creation of the Earth to 4004 BC, based on his meticulous analysis of biblical genealogies.

One of the primary Scriptural references supporting the Young Earth perspective is found in Genesis 5, which provides detailed genealogies from Adam to Noah. Genesis 5:3-32 outlines the ages of each patriarch at the time of the birth of their firstborn sons and their lifespans, creating a chronological framework used by Creationists to calculate the Earth's age.

In contrast, the Fundamentalist perspective allows for a range of interpretations regarding the age of the Earth, often accommodating both Young Earth Creationism and Old Earth Creationism. Old Earth Creationists propose a more extended timeframe, incorporating scientific evidence such as geological findings, radiometric dating, and astronomical observations.

Some Fundamentalists interpret the "days" of creation in Genesis metaphorically, suggesting that each "day" could represent vast periods. This perspective is in line with the notion that God's concept of time may differ from human understanding, allowing for a more extended interpretation of the creation account.

Another Scripture frequently cited in the Old Earth Creationist viewpoint is Psalm 90:4, which states, "For a thousand years in your sight are like a day that has just gone by, or like a watch in the night." This verse underscores the idea that time is perceived differently by God, potentially reconciling the scientific evidence suggesting an Earth much older than the Young Earth model.

Fundamentalists also consider scientific data, such as radiometric dating methods, which estimate the age of rocks and minerals. These methods suggest an Earth age of approximately 4.5 billion years, aligning more closely with the scientific consensus.

The age of the Earth remains a complex and debated topic within Creationism and Fundamentalism. While Creationists advocate for a Young Earth, dating back several thousand years, Fundamentalists embrace a broader range of interpretations, accommodating both Young Earth and Old Earth perspectives. The divergence arises from differing approaches to biblical interpretation and the incorporation of scientific evidence. Each perspective holds its unique strengths and challenges, inviting scholars and believers to engage in respectful dialogue as they seek to understand God's creative work and the mysteries of the universe.

6.3 The Formation of the Moon in Genesis

While the account in Genesis would be easy to comprehend for our ancestors in biblical times, there is, however, overwhelming evidence to suggest that the Moon was not formed, as postulated in Gn. 1:16-17. As well, describing the Moon as a "light" gives insight into the level of understanding of celestial objects in biblical times.

From a theological perspective, these verses reflect the ancient worldview of the authors, who lived in a pre-scientific era. The motivation behind mentioning the formation of the Moon is likely to emphasize God's role as the ultimate Creator of the celestial bodies and their specific functions. The mention of God creating the "lesser light to govern the night" denotes the Moon's role in providing light during the night, while the "greater light to govern the day" refers to the Sun, which provides light during the day.

The purpose of these verses is not to offer a detailed scientific explanation of the Moon's formation or its astronomical properties. Instead, it serves to highlight God's sovereignty over the cosmos and the orderliness of His creation. The text may also convey the notion that all aspects of the natural world are intricately designed and have a divine purpose, reflecting the author's religious beliefs and desire to glorify the Creator.

6.4 The Formation of the Stars in Genesis

In the book of Genesis, the account of the creation of the stars stands as a pivotal moment in the creation narrative, reflecting central theological themes and imparting profound lessons to both Creationists and Fundamentalists. As they delve into this celestial wonder, these perspectives offer unique insights that shape their beliefs and understanding of God's sovereign work.

From the Creationist perspective, Genesis 1:14-19 recounts the fourth day of creation, where God declares, "Let there be lights in the expanse of the heavens to separate the day from the night. And let them be for signs and seasons, and days and years, and let them be lights in the expanse of the heavens to give light upon the earth." Creationists emphasize that God, as the omnipotent Creator, brought the stars into existence ex nihilo, highlighting His divine power and authority over the entire cosmos. They perceive the stars as a testament to God's infinite creativity and craftsmanship, a manifestation of His glory and majesty. For Creationists, the stars also serve as a reminder of the precise order and purpose embedded in creation, showcasing God's meticulous design and sustenance of the universe.

Fundamentalists, on the other hand, regard the account of the stars' creation in Genesis 1:14-19 as a foundational element of biblical inerrancy. To them, the historical narrative in Genesis reflects the true events of creation as divinely inspired and without error. By affirming the historical accuracy of the biblical record, Fundamentalists assert the reliability of God's Word, finding assurance in the trustworthiness of Scripture. They perceive the creation of stars as a testament to God's grand plan for humanity and His redemptive purposes throughout history. Fundamentalists view the stars as a celestial clock, appointed by God to mark seasons, days, and years, and a celestial guide used by early navigators to discern their paths, symbolizing God's providential care and guidance over His creation.

Both perspectives draw central theological themes and lessons from the creation of stars in Genesis. First, the stars highlight God's transcendence and immanence, showcasing His ability to create and govern the vast cosmos while caring for the intricate details of human existence. Second, the stars reveal the beauty and diversity of God's creation, underscoring His desire for humanity to marvel at His handiwork and respond in worship and reverence. Third, the stars serve as a reminder of human insignificance in comparison to the magnificence of the Creator, fostering humility and reliance on God's wisdom and providence. Lastly, the stars offer a glimpse into God's eternal nature, as they continue to shine throughout generations, demonstrating His faithfulness and constancy in an ever-changing world.

The creation of the stars in Genesis provides Creationists and Fundamentalists with profound theological insights and valuable lessons. While Creationists find in the stars a manifestation of God's creative power and design, Fundamentalists affirm the historical accuracy and inerrancy of the biblical record. Together, they learn from the stars about God's transcendence, beauty, and faithfulness, encouraging them to embrace humility and worship in the presence of the great Creator. The account of the stars in Genesis stands as a foundational piece of the creation narrative, inviting believers of both perspectives to deepen their understanding of God and His divine purposes in the universe.

7 Scientific Creation Account

7.1 The Big Bang Theory

While Creationists and Fundamentalists would like to have you believe that the belief in The Big Bang Theory is mutually exclusive from a Christian belief, I suggest that The Big Bang Theory is an alternate view of creation, offering a modern scientific perspective on the origins of the universe. As we delve into the complexities of this cosmological model and examine its implications for our understanding of creation. While Genesis chapters 1 and 2 provide foundational accounts of creation from a theological standpoint, the Big Bang Theory presents a scientifically informed explanation that has become widely accepted among cosmologists and astrophysicists.

The creation narratives in Genesis chapters 1 and 2 hold a central place in Judeo-Christian theology, providing profound insights into the nature of God and humanity. These accounts emphasize the divine agency and intentionality behind the cosmos and the special relationship between God and humanity. The imagery of God speaking creation into existence and forming humanity from the dust of the ground conveys the theological significance of God's creative power.

The Big Bang Theory[xxxiii] proposes that the universe originated from an immensely hot and dense state approximately 13.8 billion years ago. This concept is supported by various lines of scientific evidence, including the redshift of galaxies, cosmic microwave background radiation, and the abundance of light elements. The theory suggests that the universe has been expanding ever since its inception, providing a framework for understanding the large-scale structure of the cosmos.

While the Big Bang Theory presents a scientific explanation of the universe's origins, it need not be viewed as incompatible with theological perspectives on creation. Many theologians and religious scholars have sought to harmonize scientific discoveries with spiritual insights. The recognition that science and theology address different aspects of human experience allows for a complementary understanding of the universe's origins.

The Big Bang Theory prompts theological reflections on the nature of God as the ultimate source of existence and the sustainer of the cosmos. This scientific model invites us to contemplate the mystery of creation and the divine creativity inherent in the unfolding of the universe. The idea that the universe had a definite beginning raises questions about the purpose and intentionality behind its existence, concepts that resonate with theological inquiries.

The concept of cosmic evolution, as suggested by the Big Bang Theory and subsequent scientific findings, raises questions about divine providence and the unfolding of God's plan for creation. Some theologians propose that the evolving universe can be seen as participating in God's ongoing creative work, in which both natural processes and divine agency are at play.

Understanding the Big Bang Theory and the vastness of the cosmos can have ethical and moral implications for humanity. It calls us to recognize the interconnectedness of all life forms on Earth and the responsibility we bear as stewards of the planet. This perspective encourages ethical considerations regarding environmental preservation and sustainable practices.

The Big Bang Theory invites us to contemplate God as the Author of Space and Time, the ultimate source from which all existence emerges. This theological perspective explores the transcendence and immanence of God, acknowledging the divine presence in the vastness of the cosmos and within every atom of creation.

Both theological and scientific inquiries into creation confront us with profound mystery and call us to humility. As we explore the Big Bang Theory and the ancient creation narratives, we acknowledge the limits of human understanding and the awe-inspiring vastness of the universe. This sense of humility can enrich our spiritual journey and deepen our appreciation for the divine wisdom behind creation.

The Big Bang Theory, as an alternate view of creation, provides a scientific framework for understanding the origins and evolution of the universe. While it stands as a separate discourse from the theological narratives in Genesis chapters 1 and 2, the Big Bang Theory invites us to contemplate the mystery and beauty of the cosmos. Harmonizing the insights from science and theology can enrich our understanding of creation and our place within the grand tapestry of existence. Embracing the dialogue between scientific exploration and theological reflection allows us to appreciate the wondrous interplay of divine creativity and natural processes that shape the universe we inhabit. As we humbly explore the vastness of creation, may it deepen our reverence for the divine and nurture our sense of responsibility as caretakers of this precious planet we call home.

7.2 Complex organisms took billions of years to arise

The emergence of complex organisms, including humans, from the initial event of the Big Bang represents a captivating journey of evolution and transformation that spans billions of years. It is necessary to explore the scientific view of how the intricate tapestry of life arose from the primordial conditions following the Big Bang, highlighting several examples that affirm the legitimacy of this perspective.

The Big Bang, estimated to have occurred approximately 13.8 billion years ago, marked the beginning of our universe. In its early moments, only simple particles like protons, neutrons, and electrons existed. Through processes such as nucleosynthesis in the intense heat and energy of the early universe, these particles combined to form hydrogen and helium atoms, laying the foundational elements for later cosmic evolution.

About 4.6 billion years ago, in the aftermath of stellar explosions known as supernovae, heavier elements like carbon, oxygen, and nitrogen were forged in the fiery furnaces of dying stars. These elements were then scattered into space, eventually coalescing to form the raw materials essential for life.

On Earth, life emerged approximately 3.5 to 3.8 billion years ago[xxxiv]. The early oceans and a unique set of environmental conditions provided the backdrop for the formation of simple organic molecules, possibly facilitated by energy sources such as lightning or hydrothermal vents. These molecules eventually gave rise to the first self-replicating entities, laying the groundwork for biological evolution.

The process of natural selection, proposed by Charles Darwin and supported by a wealth of empirical evidence, acts as a driving force for the evolution of life on Earth. Over vast periods, organisms that possessed advantageous traits were more likely to survive and reproduce, leading to the gradual development of more complex and specialized forms of life.

The evolutionary timeline is punctuated by key events, such as the Cambrian explosion[xxxv] around 541 million years ago when a burst of diversification led to the emergence of various animal phyla. Around 370 million years ago[xxxvi], plants transitioned from water to land, marking another significant evolutionary leap. Mammals emerged around 200 million years ago, and primates, from which humans eventually descended, appeared around 60 million years ago.

Genetics and molecular biology provide compelling evidence for the relatedness of all life on Earth. The discovery of DNA, the genetic code that carries instructions for the development and functioning of organisms, has revealed a common genetic language shared by all living beings. Comparative genomics[xxxvii] highlights the shared ancestry of humans and other species, reinforcing the view that complex organisms, including humans, emerged through a gradual and interconnected process.

The emergence of complex organisms, including humans, from the Big Bang is a scientific narrative grounded in evidence from cosmology, geology, paleontology, evolutionary biology, and genetics. From the formation of basic elements in the aftermath of the Big Bang to the emergence of self-replicating molecules and the gradual diversification of life, the journey showcases the interconnectedness and evolutionary continuity that has shaped the biological world we inhabit today.

Vast amounts of detail can be added to the overview above; although, at the end of the day, I believe with every fiber of my being that this process did not happen randomly or accidentally. At the instant of creation, God knew that one day we would exist. In my opinion, making such an assertion requires more faith than does the six days of creation model offered in Genesis.

7.3 Development of DNA from disorder

The journey from the point of the Big Bang to the intricate complexity of life as we observe today, including the existence of complex DNA[xxxviii], is a testament to the remarkable process of cosmic and biological evolution. Over the course of billions of years, a series of interconnected events, guided by fundamental physical laws and natural selection, have shaped the unfolding story of life on Earth.

The Big Bang, estimated to have occurred around 13.8 billion years ago, marked the inception of our universe. In its initial moments, only the simplest particles like protons, neutrons, and electrons existed. Through processes like nucleosynthesis in the intense heat of the early universe, these particles combined to form hydrogen and helium atoms, which eventually provided the building blocks for more complex elements in later stellar generations.

Around 4.6 billion years ago[xxxix], our solar system emerged from a cloud of gas and dust, ignited by the fusion of hydrogen in the core of a star, leading to the birth of our Sun. This event not only set the stage for the formation of our planetary system but also enabled the synthesis of heavier elements like carbon, oxygen, and nitrogen, essential for the molecular complexity of life.

The emergence of life on Earth began approximately 3.5 to 3.8 billion years ago, possibly in the form of simple organic molecules. Miller-Urey[xl] experiments in the 1950s demonstrated that the combination of gases and electrical discharges, similar to conditions on early Earth, could lead to the formation of amino acids, the building blocks of proteins. These amino acids are vital components of complex DNA.

The process of abiogenesis, the natural emergence of life from non-living matter, remains a topic of ongoing research. While the precise mechanisms are not yet fully understood, experiments have shown that under appropriate conditions, organic molecules can self-assemble and interact to form more complex structures. The RNA world hypothesis[xli] proposes that RNA[xlii], a molecule structurally related to DNA, played a crucial role in the early stages of life, as it can both store genetic information and catalyze chemical reactions.

The emergence of DNA and its evolution into complex forms can be observed through fossil records and genetic analysis. The oldest fossils of simple microbial life date back around 3.5 billion years[xliii], indicating the early presence of life on Earth. Over time, natural selection acted upon variations within populations, favoring those with traits beneficial for survival and reproduction. This gradual process of adaptation led to the diversification of life and the eventual development of complex organisms with intricate DNA.

The journey from the Big Bang to the complex DNA of the present day is a narrative of cosmic and biological evolution. The formation of elements, the emergence of our solar system, the rise of life on Earth, and the intricate process of natural selection have collectively contributed to the evolution of complexity. While the exact details of how life originated remain a topic of investigation, the evidence from various scientific disciplines supports the gradual development of DNA and the astonishing diversity of life we observe today.

It should also be noted that this process did not happen arbitrarily. At the instant of creation, God knew what the outcome would be. We did not get here by chance, or by accident.

7.4 Radiometric Dating

Radiometric dating[xliv], a powerful technique used to determine the age of rocks and minerals, has revolutionized the field of geochronology[xlv] and provides a legitimate and well-supported approach to dating Earth's history. Numerous examples and robust scientific principles contribute to the validity of radiometric dating, ensuring its reliability in determining the precise ages of geological materials.

One of the primary methods used in radiometric dating is uranium-lead dating[xlvi], which accurately measures the decay of uranium isotopes into lead over time. For instance, zircon crystals found in ancient rocks have been precisely dated using uranium-lead dating, revealing ages as old as 4.36 billion years, consistent with the estimated age of the Earth.

Another example is the use of potassium-argon dating[xlvii], a radiometric technique employed in dating volcanic rocks. The decay of potassium-40 into argon-40 allows geologists to determine the age of volcanic formations. For instance, the volcanic rocks from the Olduvai Gorge in Tanzania[xlviii], where important hominid fossils were discovered, have been dated using potassium-argon dating, providing an age estimate of approximately 1.75 million years.

Additionally, the technique of rubidium-strontium dating[xlix] is widely used to date rocks and minerals. For example, the age of the Sudbury Basin in Canada[l], a significant impact crater, has been determined using rubidium-strontium dating, yielding an age estimate of approximately 1.85 billion years.

Furthermore, the validity of radiometric dating is bolstered by its consistent application across various materials and geological formations. Dates obtained from different radiometric methods on the same rocks generally agree, providing a robust cross-validation of the results. This consistency and agreement between dating methods reinforce the legitimacy of radiometric dating as a reliable tool for determining the ages of geological samples.

Moreover, the precision and accuracy of radiometric dating have improved significantly with advances in technology and analytical techniques. Modern mass spectrometers and detectors allow for the detection of even the smallest amounts of parent and daughter isotopes[li], leading to more accurate age determinations. For example, the development of multi-collector inductively coupled plasma mass spectrometry (MC-ICP-MS[lii]) has greatly enhanced the precision and accuracy of uranium-lead dating.

Radiometric dating stands as a legitimate and well-supported scientific technique for determining the ages of geological materials. Examples such as uranium-lead dating applied to zircon crystals from ancient rocks, potassium-argon dating on volcanic formations, and rubidium-strontium dating of impact craters showcase the precision and accuracy of this method. Consistency between different radiometric methods and advancements in technology further reinforce the validity of radiometric dating. As a result, radiometric dating plays a fundamental role in unraveling the chronology of Earth's history and understanding the vast expanse of geological time.

7.5 Scientific Principles of Radiometric Dating

Radiometric dating is founded upon three fundamental principles:

Radioactive Decay: Some isotopes are unstable and undergo radioactive decay at a constant and predictable rate known as their half-life. Each radioactive isotope has a specific half-life, ranging from fractions of a second to billions of years.

Parent-Daughter Ratios: When a rock forms, it contains a known proportion of parent and daughter isotopes. As the parent isotopes decay, the proportion of parent-to-daughter isotopes changes over time, allowing scientists to determine the age of the rock.

Closed System Behavior: The material being dated must be a closed system, meaning it has not experienced any significant gain or loss of parent or daughter isotopes since its formation. This ensures that the calculated age reflects the time since the rock's formation.

Examples of Radiometric Dating Determining the Age of Earth:

Age of the Earth (Uranium-Lead Dating): Uranium-lead dating is a widely used radiometric dating method for dating the age of the Earth. By analyzing the isotopic composition of ancient rocks and minerals, scientists have estimated the age of Earth to be approximately 4.54 billion years. This groundbreaking discovery revolutionized our understanding of Earth's history and formation.

Age of the Moon (Rubidium-Strontium and Uranium-Lead Dating): Radiometric dating has been instrumental in determining the age of the Moon. Analysis of lunar rock samples collected during the Apollo missions indicated that the Moon formed approximately 4.5 billion years ago, around the same time as the Earth.

Age of Meteorites (Various Radiometric Methods): Meteorites, which are remnants of the early solar system, provide valuable insights into the age of our solar system.

Radiometric dating methods, such as uranium-lead, rubidium-strontium, and samarium-neodymium dating[liii], have been used to estimate the ages of meteorites, yielding consistent results of approximately 4.5 billion years.

Age of Terrestrial Rocks (Potassium-Argon and Argon-Argon Dating): Potassium-argon and argon-argon dating[liv] are commonly employed to date volcanic rocks and minerals on Earth. For example, radiometric dating of volcanic rocks from the Hawaiian Islands[lv] has helped establish the geological timeline of the region, shedding light on the formation and evolution of the islands over millions of years.

Radiometric dating has undergone rigorous testing and validation through cross-checking with independent dating methods, such as luminescence dating[lvi] and fossil dating[lvii]. In addition, the technique has been verified through the dating of historical events, such as volcanic eruptions with known ages. The consistent and concordant results from different isotopic systems and various rock types further support the accuracy and validity of radiometric dating.

Radiometric dating stands as a robust and reliable method for determining the age of the Earth and various rocks. The scientific principles of radioactive decay, parent-daughter ratios, and closed-system behavior underpin the validity of this dating technique. Numerous examples, such as dating the Earth, Moon, meteorites, and terrestrial rocks, have demonstrated the accuracy and credibility of radiometric dating. This technique continues to be an indispensable tool in geochronology, contributing significantly to our understanding of Earth's geological history and the evolution of the solar system.

7.6 Age of the Earth according to science

Determining the age of the Earth has been a fascinating quest for geologists and scientists, resulting in a well-established scientific consensus supported by various robust dating methods. Through extensive research and analysis, the scientific community has arrived at a legitimate estimate for the age of our planet, placing it at approximately 4.54 billion years old.

One of the primary methods used to calculate the age of the Earth is radiometric dating, particularly the dating of rocks and minerals containing radioactive isotopes. For instance, uranium-lead dating is employed to determine the age of rocks, such as zircon crystals, by measuring the decay of uranium isotopes into lead over time. This method has been applied to some of the oldest rocks on Earth, providing precise ages that align with the established age of the planet.

Another dating technique used in the determination of Earth's age is potassium-argon dating, which measures the decay of potassium-40 into argon-40 in volcanic rocks. This method has been extensively applied to various volcanic formations, and the resulting ages consistently support the estimated age of the Earth.

In addition to radiometric dating, astronomers have employed astronomical dating techniques to support the age of the Earth. For example, the analysis of meteorites and lunar samples brought back from the Moon during the Apollo missions has provided valuable information about the early history of our solar system. By dating these extraterrestrial materials, scientists can infer the approximate age of the Earth and the solar system, yielding results that are consistent with radiometric dating estimates.

Furthermore, the study of Earth's magnetic field has revealed periodic reversals[lviii] in polarity recorded in rocks. By comparing these magnetic reversals with the known polarity sequence from the present day, scientists can estimate the time it took to generate the observed magnetic history. These estimates support the long-standing age of the Earth.

Additionally, research into the rate of sediment accumulation[lix] in the ocean and the accumulation of salt in the seas[lx] provides further evidence for the age of the Earth. By measuring the sedimentation rates and salt content in the oceans, scientists have calculated the approximate time required for the current levels to accumulate, supporting the age of our planet.

The age of the Earth, estimated at approximately 4.54 billion years, is a well-established scientific consensus based on multiple dating methods and extensive research. Radiometric dating, astronomical dating, studies of Earth's magnetic field, and sediment accumulation rates all converge to support this legitimate view of our planet's age. The scientific community continues to refine and improve dating techniques, providing even greater confidence in the established age of the Earth.

7.7 Alternate view of Moon creation

The Moon, Earth's only natural satellite, has fascinated scientists for generations. Determining its origin is essential for comprehending the formation and evolution of the Earth-Moon system. The Giant Impact Theory[lxi] proposes that a massive collision between Earth and a Mars-sized celestial body, often referred to as "Theia," led to the formation of the Moon.

The Giant Impact Theory suggests that approximately 4.5 billion years ago, during the Late Heavy Bombardment[lxii] period, a collision between early Earth and a planetesimal, Theia, occurred. This impact resulted in a massive debris disk and eventual accretion of material to form the Moon. Key elements of the hypothesis include:

1. **Collision:** Theia, a Mars-sized body, collided with Earth at a glancing angle, releasing an enormous amount of energy and ejecting a significant portion of Earth's mantle and Theia's core and mantle into space.

2. **Debris Disk Formation:** The ejected material from the collision formed a hot and dense debris disk around Earth.

3. **Moon Formation:** Over time, the debris disk coalesced to form the Moon through accretion. The Moon eventually reached a stable orbit around Earth.

Supporting Evidence for the Giant Impact Theory:

1. **Lunar Rocks and Isotope Analysis:** Lunar samples brought back by the Apollo missions have similar isotopic compositions to Earth, supporting a common origin. However, some isotopic differences have been found, suggesting a minor contribution from Theia.

2. **Lunar Orbiter and Earth-Moon Similarities:** The Moon's composition[lxiii] is significantly different from that of other planets in the solar system but shares similarities with Earth's mantle. Additionally, the Moon's iron core is smaller than expected, consistent with Theia's core merging with Earth's.

3. **Angular Momentum and Spin:** The Moon's current orbital and rotational characteristics are consistent with those predicted by the Giant Impact Theory.

4. **Numerical Simulations:** Computer simulations have successfully recreated the formation of the Moon from a giant impact, showing the plausibility of the hypothesis.

The Giant Impact Theory has significant implications for our understanding of lunar and planetary evolution:

1. **Early Earth's Environment:** The Moon's formation played a crucial role in the early evolution of Earth, affecting its rotation rate, tides, and potentially the development of life.

2. **Moon's Formation Timeline:** The Giant Impact Theory helps explain the Moon's relatively rapid formation compared to other theories, which is consistent with the ages of lunar rocks and the early solar system.

3. **Planetary Accretion and Composition:** The collision that led to the Moon's formation reflects the dynamic processes involved in planetary accretion in the early solar system.

The Giant Impact Theory stands as the most widely held and supported theory for the formation of the Moon. The accumulation of geological evidence, isotope analysis, lunar sample studies, and numerical simulations has reinforced its credibility. This hypothesis provides a comprehensive and consistent framework for understanding the formation of the Moon and its role in shaping the early Earth-Moon system. Ongoing research continues to refine our knowledge of this momentous event in the history of the solar system, further deepening our understanding of planetary formation and evolution.

7.8 Creation of stars from a scientific perspective

The formation of stars is a captivating subject in astrophysics, shedding light on the intricacies of the universe's birth and evolution. Scientifically, stars emerge from vast interstellar clouds of gas and dust, undergoing a complex process that extends over millions of years. This perspective is considered legitimate for several compelling reasons, supported by empirical evidence and theoretical models.

Firstly, observational data from various space telescopes, such as the Hubble Space Telescope[lxiv] and the Spitzer Space Telescope[lxv], provide astronomers with stunning images of stellar nurseries, where stars are born. These images show dense regions of gas and dust known as molecular clouds, where the gravitational collapse initiates the star formation process. The presence of these molecular clouds, along with protostellar objects in various stages of development, serves as visual proof of the scientific explanation for star creation.

Secondly, scientific models, particularly the widely accepted theory of gravitational collapse[lxvi], offer a robust framework to understand star formation. According to this theory, molecular clouds, held together by gravitational forces, fragment into smaller clumps. These clumps continue to collapse under gravity, leading to the formation of cores, and eventually, protostars. The conservation of angular momentum and energy within the collapsing cloud also explains the emergence of a rotating disk around the protostar, a crucial step in the formation process. These models align with the observed properties of young stellar objects and reinforce the scientific legitimacy of star creation.

Additionally, astronomical observations of star-forming regions reveal the presence of various phenomena closely associated with the star-formation process. For instance, the detection of powerful outflows and jets of material from protostars, known as Herbig-Haro objects, is consistent with theoretical predictions of the mass-accretion phase during star birth. The appearance of these Herbig-Haro objects[lxvii] offers a compelling line of evidence supporting the scientific perspective of star formation.

Furthermore, advances in computational simulations have allowed scientists to model and reproduce the intricate dynamics of star formation in virtual environments. These simulations successfully reproduce observed characteristics of molecular clouds, the collapse of cores, and the subsequent formation of stars. The convergence between these simulations and observational data reinforces the legitimacy of the scientific approach to understanding star creation.

Lastly, the life cycle of stars, as predicted by stellar evolution models[lxviii], matches the observed distribution of stars across different stages of their existence. From protostars to main-sequence stars, and ultimately to red giants or supernovae, the progression of stars through their life cycles is in harmony with the scientific understanding of stellar formation.

The scientific perspective on the creation of stars is supported by a plethora of evidence from astronomical observations, theoretical models, and computational simulations. The presence of molecular clouds, the existence of protostellar objects, and the emergence of rotating disks around young stars provide compelling visual evidence. The gravitational collapse theory, coupled with the presence of Herbig-Haro objects, corroborates the theoretical framework for star formation. Additionally, the successful replication of observed phenomena in computational simulations solidifies the scientific legitimacy of this perspective. Finally, the accurate alignment between stellar evolution models and observed distributions of stars further reinforces the scientific understanding of star creation. As such, the scientific perspective on the formation of stars stands as a legitimate and well-supported explanation within the realm of astrophysics.

7.9 The Size of the Universe

Understanding the size of the universe has been a profound challenge for astronomers and cosmologists throughout history. However, modern scientific investigations have provided compelling evidence supporting the notion of an immensely vast and expanding cosmos.

The first line of evidence supporting the vastness of the universe comes from the observations of distant galaxies. Telescopes, both ground-based and space-based, have allowed astronomers to peer deep into space, revealing an abundance of galaxies scattered across the cosmos. The Hubble Ultra-Deep Field[lxix], captured by the Hubble Space Telescope, showcases thousands of galaxies, each comprising billions of stars. The sheer number and distribution of these galaxies suggest that the universe is spatially extensive and contains billions of light-years of space.

Another piece of evidence is the redshift observed in the light from distant galaxies. The redshift is a phenomenon where the light from a distant object appears to be shifted towards longer wavelengths due to the expansion of space. Edwin Hubble's[lxx] groundbreaking work in the 1920s demonstrated a clear correlation between the distance to galaxies and their redshift, indicating that the universe is expanding. The discovery of the cosmic microwave background radiation[lxxi] further reinforced this notion, as it serves as an echo of the Big Bang, the event that marks the birth of our universe. The redshift observations and the cosmic microwave background lend strong support to the idea that the universe is not only vast but also constantly expanding.

Cosmic inflation theory[lxxii] offers yet another compelling example of the universe's large-scale structure. According to this theory, the universe underwent a period of rapid expansion just moments after the Big Bang. This inflationary phase explains why distant regions of the universe, which appear disconnected today, have similar properties such as temperature and density. The homogeneity and isotropy observed in the cosmic microwave background radiation provide additional evidence for this inflationary scenario, reinforcing the notion that the universe is much larger than what we can currently observe.

The discovery of cosmic voids further emphasizes the vastness of the universe. Voids are vast regions in space that contain significantly fewer galaxies compared to the surrounding regions. The existence of these cosmic voids[lxxiii] and the large-scale structure of galaxy superclusters[lxxiv] provide evidence for the spatial extent of the universe beyond what our telescopes can currently detect.

Lastly, the concept of the observable universe, which is the portion of the universe accessible to our observations due to the finite speed of light, bolsters the idea of the universe's enormous size. The observable universe[lxxv] is estimated to have a radius of approximately 46.5 billion light-years, providing a glimpse of the vast cosmic expanse beyond our reach.

The scientific perspective on the size of the universe is well-supported by multiple lines of evidence. Observations of distant galaxies, the redshift of light from these galaxies, and the cosmic microwave background radiation all point to the vastness and expansion of the cosmos. The inflationary model explains the large-scale homogeneity of the universe, while the presence of cosmic voids highlights the significant spatial extent beyond what we can currently observe. Additionally, the notion of the observable universe sets a limit on our reach within this vast cosmic arena. Together, these examples contribute to the legitimacy of the scientific understanding of the immense size of the universe.

7.10 The speed at which light travels supports the age of the Universe

The speed of light[lxxvi], a fundamental constant in physics denoted by 'c,' plays a crucial role in supporting the scientific determination of the age of the universe. Several well-established principles and empirical evidence underpin the legitimacy of this view, highlighting the relationship between the speed of light and the vast expanse of time since the Big Bang.

Firstly, the cosmic microwave background radiation (CMB) provides a pivotal example of how the speed of light enables us to gauge the age of the universe. The CMB is a relic radiation from the early universe, dating back to approximately 380,000 years after the Big Bang when the universe became transparent to light. This radiation was emitted from a primordial plasma and has since cooled, stretching its wavelength from initially being in the visible spectrum to microwave frequencies today. By measuring the temperature and characteristics of the CMB, astronomers can determine the time elapsed since its emission. The constancy of the speed of light allows scientists to accurately calculate the vast distance this radiation has traveled and, consequently, the age of the universe.

Secondly, the concept of the observable universe relies heavily on the speed of light. As light travels at a finite speed, the universe we can observe is limited by the distance light has had time to reach us since the Big Bang. Thus, our observations can only extend as far as the distance light could have traveled during the age of the universe. The vastness of the observable universe further reinforces the immense age of our cosmos.

The distance to remote astronomical objects, such as galaxies and quasars, provides yet another example of how the speed of light contributes to our understanding of the universe's age. Astronomers use the redshift of light from these objects, caused by the expansion of the universe, to determine their distance from Earth. By measuring these distances, scientists can trace the expansion of the universe backward in time, eventually leading to the moment of the Big Bang. The speed of light is integral to calculating these distances and, consequently, the age of the universe.

Furthermore, time delay in the arrival of light from distant cosmic phenomena, such as supernovae and gamma ray bursts[lxxvii], allows astronomers to infer the vastness of space and the resulting age of the universe. By comparing the observed and expected times of arrival for light emitted by these events, scientists can deduce the distances involved, which ultimately contribute to our understanding of the cosmic timescale.

The speed of light is a foundational constant that underpins the scientific determination of the age of the universe. From analyzing the cosmic microwave background radiation to understanding the concept of the observable universe, the speed of light enables us to gauge the immense temporal expanse since the Big Bang. It plays a critical role in measuring distances to distant cosmic objects, allowing scientists to trace the expansion of the universe backward in time. Additionally, the time delay in the arrival of light from distant phenomena further solidifies the legitimacy of using the speed of light to support the age of the universe from a scientific perspective.

8 Adam and Eve

8.1 Creationist and Fundamentalist Perspective

The story of Adam and Eve, nestled within the opening chapters of Genesis, holds profound theological significance for both Creationists and Fundamentalists. These perspectives provide distinct insights into the context, themes, and lessons of this foundational narrative, exploring the origins of humanity, sin, and redemption.

From the Creationist viewpoint, the story of Adam and Eve serves as a pivotal event that underscores the divine origin of humanity and the subsequent fall from grace. The narrative unfolds in the Garden of Eden, where God creates Adam from the dust of the ground and breathes life into him (Genesis 2:7). Creationists emphasize the literal interpretation of these events, portraying Adam and Eve as the first human beings directly created by God's creative act. This perspective underscores the uniqueness of human creation and the direct relationship between God and humanity.

Genesis 2:15-17 reveals God's command to Adam regarding the Tree of the Knowledge of Good and Evil, instructing him not to eat from it. Creationists regard this command as a test of obedience and free will. Subsequently, Eve is created from Adam's rib, further underscoring the unity and companionship between man and woman. The serpent's deception and the ensuing disobedience of Adam and Eve lead to the introduction of sin into the world, and Creationists emphasize the consequences of this disobedience as the foundation for the need for redemption through Jesus Christ.

The Fundamentalist perspective aligns with the Creationist interpretation of the events surrounding Adam and Eve while emphasizing the inerrancy and historical accuracy of the biblical account. Fundamentalists assert that the story of Adam and Eve is not allegorical but rather a record of historical events that shaped the course of human history. This narrative establishes the context for humanity's fallen state, demonstrating the reality of sin's impact on the relationship between God and mankind.

Genesis 3:6 captures the pivotal moment when Eve partakes of the forbidden fruit and shares it with Adam. Fundamentalists stress that this act of disobedience introduced sin into the world and led to a rupture in the harmonious relationship between humanity and God. The resulting consequences, including the expulsion from the Garden of Eden and the introduction of pain and suffering, underline the serious ramifications of human rebellion. Fundamentalists also view this narrative as a foreshadowing of the need for a Savior, culminating in God's promise of redemption through the seed of the woman (Genesis 3:15).

The story of Adam and Eve in Genesis holds profound theological significance for both Creationists and Fundamentalists. As Creationists emphasize the direct creation of humanity by God and the fall from grace, Fundamentalists underscore the historical accuracy and inerrancy of the narrative, emphasizing the impact of sin on humanity's relationship with God. Together, these perspectives provide believers with a foundational understanding of human origins, the nature of sin, and the profound need for redemption through Jesus Christ.

8.2 Theological perspective

The narrative of Adam and Eve in the Book of Genesis stands as a pivotal account within the theological framework of Christianity, offering profound insights into human origins, sin, and divine redemption. In Genesis 2, God molds the first human, Adam, from the dust of the earth, imbuing him with life (Genesis 2:7). Subsequently, God places Adam in the Garden of Eden, an earthly paradise brimming with abundance and perfection (Genesis 2:8-9). Recognizing Adam's solitude, God fashions Eve from one of Adam's ribs, establishing a unique bond between the two as partners and companions (Genesis 2:21-22).

From a Catholic perspective, the story of Adam and Eve is understood both allegorically and theologically. Catholics perceive these primordial figures as emblematic of all humanity, signifying the unity and interconnectedness of the human race. The Fall of Adam and Eve, marked by their disobedience in partaking of the forbidden fruit from the tree of knowledge (Genesis 3:6), is viewed as the introduction of original sin into human nature. This event disrupted the harmony between humanity and God, leading to a state of estrangement and moral imperfection. The Catholic Church teaches that this original sin necessitates the redemption provided by Jesus Christ, who is referred to as the "New Adam." Christ's sacrificial death and resurrection offer humanity the opportunity to reconcile with God and regain divine grace.

In contrast, the Creationist perspective, particularly within Young Earth Creationism, interprets the Adam and Eve story as a historical and literal event. This viewpoint asserts the belief in a young Earth, approximately 6,000 to 10,000 years old, and contends that the account in Genesis describes the actual creation of Adam and Eve as the first humans. The Fall, driven by their defiance of God's command, is viewed as the catalyst for humanity's inherent sinful nature. Creationists reject evolutionary explanations, advocating for a literal interpretation of the Genesis narrative as foundational to understanding human origins and sin.

The Fundamentalist interpretation closely aligns with Creationism but emphasizes a strict, unwavering commitment to the literal interpretation of the Bible. Fundamentalists reject scientific theories and place the story of Adam and Eve at the core of their belief system, asserting that these biblical accounts provide a comprehensive understanding of human origins, morality, and the divine-human relationship. The Fall of Adam and Eve is considered the foundational event that introduced sin into the world, shaping humanity's fallen state and need for salvation.

The narrative of Adam and Eve in Genesis holds diverse interpretations from different Christian perspectives. The Catholic view treats the story as a theological allegory, emphasizing human unity, the introduction of original sin, and the necessity of redemption through Christ. Creationist perspectives, such as Young Earth Creationism, regard the narrative as a historical event that shapes views on human origins and sin. Fundamentalist interpretations closely align with Creationism, focusing on the literal reading of the Bible and the central significance of the Adam and Eve narrative for human existence and spirituality. Each perspective illuminates distinct facets of the story's theological and philosophical implications, enriching the ongoing discourse on the nature of humanity, sin, and divine grace.

8.3 Literal interpretation brings about concerns

The account of Cain and his wife in Genesis raises both theological and scientific inquiries that offer insights into biblical interpretation and the complexities of early human history. The narrative begins with the creation of Adam and Eve, whom Genesis 2:8-25 presents as the first human couple placed in the Garden of Eden.

The subsequent generations, involving the birth of Cain and Abel and the appearance of Cain's wife, have generated questions about the origin of Cain's spouse and the nature of human relationships in the context of the early biblical narrative.

From a theological perspective, the biblical narrative of Cain's wife prompts reflection on the broader context of early human existence. The Genesis narrative provides an overview of essential events, focusing on key figures in God's redemptive plan. While the text doesn't explicitly detail how Cain's wife emerged, theologians have proposed various interpretive frameworks.

A literal reading of the text in Genesis 4:17 would imply that Cain married his sister. One perspective posits that the initial generations following Adam and Eve may have intermarried with siblings or other close relatives due to the absence of a larger human population at that time. Such unions would have been permissible due to the absence of prohibitions against close kin relationships in these early stages of human history.

Theological discussions often acknowledge that the purpose of the Genesis narrative is to convey theological truths rather than provide exhaustive historical and scientific accounts. The narrative emphasizes the consequences of human choices, the effects of sin, and the unfolding of God's plan of redemption.

The focus is on spiritual and moral themes rather than comprehensive historical details. Approaching the narrative with this theological lens highlights its broader messages while recognizing that specifics about early human relationships may remain elusive.

From a scientific perspective, the question of Cain's wife can be considered in light of anthropological and genetic insights. The scenario of early human populations involving intermarriage among close relatives aligns with models of small, isolated groups that populated early human history. Genetic studies indicate that small populations can lead to genetic bottlenecks and a degree of inbreeding, which might be reflected in the biblical account. However, genetic diversity would have increased as human populations grew and migrated over time.

Addressing the question of where Cain's wife came from also invites exploration of the narrative's cultural context. Ancient Near Eastern societies often interwove myth and history, making it challenging to discern exact historical details. The narrative's primary intent is to communicate theological and moral lessons, rather than serve as a comprehensive historical record.

The account of Cain and his wife in Genesis exemplifies the complex interplay between theology, science, and historical interpretation. Theological considerations prompt reflection on the theological truths conveyed in the narrative, highlighting themes of human choice, sin, and God's redemptive plan. Scientific insights offer perspectives on early human history, genetic diversity, and cultural contexts that can enhance our understanding of the narrative's background. As believers engage with these questions, they navigate the delicate balance between the narrative's theological significance and the broader complexities of historical and scientific inquiry.

8.4 Adam and Eve as archetypal figures

The narrative of Adam and Eve, as recounted in the Book of Genesis, provides a rich canvas for theological reflection and interpretation. Beyond historical and literal perspectives, the archetypal approach to understanding Adam and Eve unveils layers of symbolism and meaning that transcend time and culture. In Genesis 2, God forms Adam from the dust of the earth and breathes life into him (Genesis 2:7). Eve, the first woman, is then fashioned from one of Adam's ribs, signifying their profound connection and shared humanity (Genesis 2:21-22).

The archetypal interpretation of Adam and Eve invites readers to consider these figures as universal symbols that encapsulate fundamental aspects of human experience. Adam, whose name in Hebrew means "man," embodies the collective essence of humanity. He represents the struggle, aspirations, and choices that define the human condition. Eve, whose name signifies "life," embodies the nurturing and life-giving aspects of humanity, encompassing both the feminine principle and the essence of creation. This archetypal reading elevates Adam and Eve from mere historical characters to enduring symbols of humanity's complexities and potential.

Furthermore, the archetypal approach delves into the thematic layers of the narrative. The Garden of Eden, often interpreted as a paradisiacal realm, can be seen as a symbol of innocence, unity with creation, and a harmonious relationship with the divine. The serpent, often associated with temptation, embodies the forces of deceit and moral struggle. The pivotal moment of the Fall, where Adam and Eve partake of the forbidden fruit, can be understood as a universal allegory for the human inclination towards self-centeredness and the moral tensions inherent in free will.

This perspective holds relevance beyond specific religious traditions, resonating with diverse cultures and philosophies. The archetypal interpretation of Adam and Eve underscores the shared narratives that humanity carries across time and space, transcending the boundaries of religious affiliation. By recognizing the narrative as a source of symbolic wisdom, readers gain a deeper understanding of the human condition and the universal struggle between moral choices and consequences.

In contrast to a purely literal view, the archetypal understanding of Adam and Eve opens the door to interdisciplinary explorations. Psychology, literature, art, and philosophy find resonance in these archetypal figures, offering avenues for reflection on human identity, relationships, and ethical dilemmas. By embracing the archetypal lens, the narrative becomes a source of ongoing dialogue, inviting diverse interpretations and reflections that enrich the understanding of the human journey.

The archetypal approach to Adam and Eve's story illuminates its enduring significance as a symbolically rich narrative. Beyond historical or literal interpretations, this perspective enriches our comprehension of human experience, moral choices, and the complexity of relationships. By recognizing Adam and Eve as archetypal figures, readers engage in a timeless exploration of human identity and the universal quest for meaning.

All things considered, this view, or the Catholic perspective, would be the cleanest way to resolve the issue of Cain having relations with his sister/wife in Genesis 4:17.

9 Creationist and Fundamentalist view of the Flood

9.1 Events that led up to the Genesis Flood

The events leading up to the Flood account in Genesis serve as a critical prelude to a profound cataclysmic event that holds significant theological implications for Jews and Christians. These perspectives provide unique insights into the context and scriptural foundations that set the stage for the global deluge.

From the Creationist standpoint, the sequence of events leading to the Flood is framed within a literal and historical framework, emphasizing the divine authority of Scripture. The narrative begins with the descendants of Adam and Eve, tracing the genealogical line in Genesis 5. As generations pass, the sinful nature of humanity becomes increasingly evident, and God's patience wears thin. Genesis 6:5-7 attests to this decline, stating, "The Lord saw that the wickedness of man was great in the earth and that every intention of the thoughts of his heart was only evil continually. And the Lord regretted that he had made man on the earth, and it grieved him to his heart."

Creationists see the rise of wickedness as a direct consequence of human rebellion against God's commands. God chooses Noah, a righteous man, to carry out a divine plan of salvation. The construction of the ark, detailed in Genesis 6:14-22, becomes a testimony to Noah's faith and obedience. The context underscores the Creator's justice and mercy, as well as the imperative for humanity to heed divine warnings and repent.

From the Fundamentalist perspective, the events before the Flood underscore the gravity of sin and the sovereignty of God.

Fundamentalists hold to a literal interpretation of Scripture, viewing the genealogies in Genesis 5 as historical records that provide a chronology of the pre-Flood era. The degradation of human morality and the proliferation of violence become clear indications of a world spiraling into moral decay.

Fundamentalists find an additional layer of context in the genealogies of Genesis 5, which provide the lifespans of the patriarchs. For instance, Methuselah, the oldest recorded person in Scripture, lived for 969 years before dying shortly before the Flood (Genesis 5:27). This extended lifespan serves as a poignant reminder of God's patience, offering ample opportunity for repentance and redemption. The narrative emphasizes the inevitability of divine judgment when humanity strays from God's moral order.

Both perspectives concur on the divine verdict of a worldwide Flood, as recorded in Genesis 7:11-24. The convergence of sin, judgment, and salvation culminates in this event, serving as a powerful reminder of God's holiness and the consequences of rebellion. For Creationists, the Flood stands as a pivotal historical event validating the reliability of Scripture, while for Fundamentalists, it underscores the need for a righteous response to God's moral commandments.

The events leading up to the Flood account in Genesis hold significant theological weight for Jews and Christians alike. The narrative serves as a cautionary tale, highlighting the ramifications of unchecked sin and God's unchanging standards. From these perspectives, the events underscore humanity's need for repentance and redemption, as well as the enduring relevance of the biblical account for contemporary discussions on morality, judgment, and divine grace.

9.2 The task given to Noah

According to the Scriptural account in Genesis 5:32, Noah reached the notable age of 500 years when he fathered Shem, Ham, and Japheth. Following this event, God bestowed upon Noah the divine mandate to construct the ark after the birth and marriage of his three children, as recorded in Genesis 6:18. It is also documented in Genesis 7:6 that Noah was 600 years old when the Great Flood began.

Considering the Biblical records that highlight the remarkable longevity of individuals, with some living well beyond 700 years, in order to give Noah a reasonable starting point to construct the ark, it would be generous to assume that all three of Noah's children were married by the age of 25. Under this presumption, the construction of the ark would have been accomplished in a period of roughly 75 years by individuals who possessed no prior experience in naval architecture.

It is worthy to note that the materials to construct the ark, as specified in Genesis 6:14-15, would have been "gopher wood, reeds, and pitch, both on the exterior and interior", there is no mention of any other component which would be used to construct the ark—certainly not metal. It is also important to keep in mind that the dimensions of the ark in Genesis 6:15 indicates that the ark would have resembled a rectangle which is perhaps, not an optimum shape for a ship.

Remarkably, there is no Scriptural indication that Noah possessed any prior proficiency in shipbuilding. The sole reference to Noah's occupation in Genesis 9:20 portrays him as a tiller of the soil or a farmer. Thus, the prospect emerges of a husbandman and his familial entourage embarking on the colossal endeavor of constructing the most prodigious wooden vessel in history.

As they sustained themselves with sustenance during this herculean endeavor, Noah, his spouse, his three sons, and their wives would have confronted the extraordinary task of crafting the necessary tools for resource extraction and ark construction. They were compelled to procure and collect the gopher wood, reeds, and pitch required for the vessel's assembly. Simultaneously, they had to cultivate and gather sufficient food to sustain themselves and the diverse animal life residing within the ark throughout an undisclosed temporal interval, which, as later revealed, endured for a full year, according to the Scriptural narrative in Genesis.

Moreover, these eight individuals faced the daunting duty of procuring, accommodating, and arranging two of every kind of animal, a feat addressed in Genesis 6:17-22. This assemblage of responsibilities appears as an immensely formidable task for a mere octet of individuals to accomplish within the confined timeframe of perhaps 75 years or less, particularly considering their lack of prior expertise in shipbuilding and the scarcity of the tools required for resource extraction and ark fabrication. Notably, there is no Scriptural indication that God provided direct assistance in the physical construction of the ark, beyond the divine instructions regarding its dimensions.

To add to the magnitude of this endeavor, as if the task before Noah and his family was not substantial enough already, in Genesis 7:1-5, *one week preceding the onset of the flood*, Noah received divine instructions to gather an additional seven pairs of "clean"[lxxviii] animals and birds of each kind". Given the extensive list of clean animals and birds, this certainly would have been an unwelcome surprise that needed to be accomplished in what would appear to be an impossible timeframe.

9.3 The Ice Age After The Flood

The assertion made by some Creationists regarding the occurrence of an Ice Age 4,300 years ago as an explanation for the water involved in the flood finds little support in established scientific research and geological evidence. The concept of an Ice Age involves prolonged periods of widespread glaciation characterized by extensive ice sheets covering vast portions of the Earth's surface, leading to significant climate changes and alterations in sea levels. The geological record and various scientific disciplines, such as glaciology and paleoclimatology[lxxix], provide compelling evidence for the occurrence of multiple Ice Ages throughout Earth's history, but these events took place over much longer timescales, not within the relatively brief timeframe posited by the Flood narrative.

Fundamentalist interpretations often rely on a literal reading of biblical texts, including the Flood account in Genesis. However, it is essential to distinguish between theological narratives and scientific explanations. While the Bible offers valuable insights into matters of faith and morality, it is not intended as a scientific textbook. Interpreting religious narratives as a substitute for well-established scientific findings can lead to misunderstandings and misinterpretations.

While religious beliefs and perspectives on creation have their place in society, conflating them with well-established scientific knowledge can hinder efforts to address pressing global challenges like climate change. Acknowledging the distinction between religious interpretations and scientific evidence is crucial for fostering a well-informed and evidence-based understanding of the world we inhabit.

Attributing the flood and its water to an Ice Age 4,300 years ago lacks credible scientific support. It is essential to approach religious narratives and scientific explanations with appropriate discernment and to recognize the valuable role that scientific research plays in understanding our planet and addressing the urgent challenges posed by climate change. Only through a comprehensive and collaborative approach that respects both scientific knowledge and religious beliefs can we endeavor to safeguard the future of our planet and its inhabitants.

9.4 The Land Bridge to Australia

The belief among some Creationists that animals aboard Noah's Ark eventually migrated to various parts of the world, including Australia, via a land bridge, raises intriguing questions concerning the plausibility of such scenarios and the supporting evidence from scientific and Scriptural perspectives.

Firstly, there is no empirical evidence supporting the notion that animals from the Ark's journey reached Australia via a land bridge. The concept of a land bridge is often invoked to explain the dispersal of species across distant continents during various geological epochs. However, such an explanation encounters significant challenges in the case of post-Flood animal migration. Geological and paleontological evidence indicates that Australia has been isolated from other landmasses for tens of millions of years, presenting difficulties in reconciling the timeline of land bridge formation with the post-Flood period as envisioned by some Fundamentalists and Creationists.

Concerning the migration of animals to North and South America from Mount Ararat, Creationists and Fundamentalist explanations often invoke additional land bridges or "catastrophic plate tectonics." The latter proposes that the massive geological upheavals during the Flood event led to rapid continental movements and created temporary land connections between distant regions. However, this idea remains speculative and lacks robust empirical support.

The explanation of "catastrophic plate tectonics" faces multiple challenges from the scientific community. Plate tectonics, as currently understood, involves the slow and continuous movement of Earth's lithospheric plates[lxxx] over millions of years, leading to phenomena such as earthquakes, mountain formation, and the opening and closing of ocean basins. The notion of rapid, cataclysmic plate movements during the Flood period contradicts the well-established principles of plate tectonics and lacks substantive geological evidence.

From a Scriptural perspective, the Bible does not provide detailed accounts of how animals dispersed across the continents after the Flood. The narrative in Genesis suggests that the Ark eventually came to rest on the mountains of Ararat, but it does not offer specific information regarding the subsequent migration of animals to far-flung regions.

It is essential to recognize that religious beliefs and scientific theories operate within distinct realms. While the biblical narrative of Noah's Ark is a sacred account cherished by believers, scientific understanding relies on empirical evidence and the rigorous testing of hypotheses. Attempting to merge these two domains, such as explaining animal migration patterns through "catastrophic plate tectonics," can lead to challenges in reconciling well-established scientific knowledge with theological interpretations.

The idea that animals from the Ark's voyage reached Australia or other distant regions via land bridges or "catastrophic plate tectonics" lacks substantial evidence from both scientific and Scriptural perspectives. Recognizing and respecting the distinct nature of religious beliefs and scientific inquiry is essential in fostering a nuanced and informed understanding of the world around us.

9.5 The concept of "Kind"

In the realm of religious discourse, "kind" holds a paramount significance for Fundamentalist and Creationist believers, since the number of "kinds" determined the number of animals that could fit on the ark. Certainly, not all 8.75 million species[lxxxi] could fit on the ark, so "kind" is considered the subset which could potentially fit on the ark. Rooted in a strict interpretation of sacred texts, Fundamentalists and Creationists view the concept of "kind" as a foundational principle that governs the diversity of life and the boundaries set by the divine order.

From a Fundamentalist and Creationist standpoint, "kind" denotes the original and distinct forms of life created by the divine force, as articulated in the sacred texts. These kinds, perceived as fixed categories, serve as a basis for understanding the boundaries of creation. Fundamentalists and Creationists assert that God created various "kinds" during the process of creation, and each "kind" possesses its unique characteristics, which cannot be transgressed or intermingled.

In Genesis 1:24-25, "And God said, 'Let the land produce living creatures according to their kinds: the livestock, the creatures that move along the ground, and the wild animals, each according to its kind.' And it was so."

This verse emphasizes God's creation of various kinds of living beings and vegetation, each distinct and self-contained. Fundamentalists and Creationists interpret these references to reinforce the idea that God intentionally designed distinct kinds, and there are limitations on the intermingling of these forms.

While Fundamentalists and Creationists generally adhere to a strict interpretation of "kind," discrepancies may arise when it comes to identifying the precise boundaries between different kinds, especially when considering scientific discoveries and taxonomical classifications. Scientific knowledge has revealed evolutionary relationships and common ancestry among various species, challenging the notion of fixed kinds.

Some scholars interpret this metaphorical language as a means to illustrate the diversity of creation emerging from a singular divine source.

From a Fundamentalist and Creationist perspective, the term "kind" holds a critical role in understanding the boundaries and diversity of God's creation. While scriptural references consistently emphasize distinct kinds, potential inconsistencies arise when reconciling religious interpretations with evolving scientific knowledge. Nonetheless, the concept of "kind" remains a cornerstone in Fundamentalist and Creationist theology, reflecting the steadfast belief in the divine order and the sanctity of creation.

9.5.1 The distinction between the word "kind" and "species"

The story of Noah's Ark, found in various religious texts such as the Bible and the Quran, holds immense significance for Jewish, Muslim and Christian believers. There is a crucial importance of distinguishing "kinds" and "species" from a Fundamentalist and Creationist perspective, specifically concerning the animals aboard Noah's Ark. Fundamentalists and Creationists maintain that recognizing this differentiation is essential to understanding the feasibility and implications of the Ark's preservation of biodiversity during the great flood.

According to the Biblical account in Genesis 6-9, God instructed Noah to construct an Ark to preserve representatives of each "kind" of land-dwelling animal during the global flood. In this context, a "kind" is believed to encompass a broader category than the contemporary scientific notion of a species. Fundamentalists and Creationists assert that God, in His divine wisdom, chose to preserve the genetic potential of various "kinds" on the Ark, from which all the diversity of life we see today eventually emerged.

In contrast to the concept of "kinds," the term "species" holds specific significance in scientific classifications. In modern biology, a species is defined as a group of organisms capable of interbreeding and producing fertile offspring. It represents a more narrowly defined category based on observable morphological and genetic characteristics. For Fundamentalists and Creationists, understanding the distinction between "kinds" and "species" is essential for reconciling the religious narrative with scientific inquiry, particularly when it comes to addressing the preservation of biodiversity on the Ark.

Fundamentalists and Creationists argue that the preservation of "kinds" rather than each individual "species" significantly impacts the feasibility of Noah's Ark. Advocates of this perspective contend that a relatively small number of "kinds" could represent the genetic potential for the vast array of species we observe today. This view implies that the diversity we see within certain animal groups (e.g., dog breeds) arose through post-flood processes of adaptation and speciation, rather than requiring every modern species to have been present on the Ark.

Critics have raised concerns regarding the sheer diversity of life on Earth and its apparent incompatibility with the Ark's capacity. Fundamentalists and Creationists, in response, point to the adaptive capabilities and genetic variability within "kinds" as the key mechanisms driving speciation and diversification post-flood. They believe that the potential for significant genetic variation within a "kind" would allow for the emergence of various species in the post-flood world.

For Fundamentalists and Creationists, the distinction between "kinds" and "species" in Noah's Ark is not merely an academic debate but carries significant theological implications. By recognizing the concept of "kinds," Fundamentalists and Creationists emphasize God's providence in preserving the building blocks of life during the flood, from which all living creatures arose. This perspective reinforces their belief in God's overarching design and the sanctity of His divine plan for creation.

Distinguishing "kinds" from "species" is of paramount importance to Fundamentalists and Creationists when discussing Noah's Ark and its implications for biodiversity. By understanding "kinds" as broader categories encompassing the genetic potential of life forms, Fundamentalists and Creationists reconcile the narrative of the Ark with scientific considerations, offering an interpretation that underscores God's providential care and divine design. As an essential aspect of their theological worldview, the distinction between "kinds" and "species" in the Ark narrative reaffirms the central role of God's sovereignty in the preservation and development of life on Earth.

9.5.2 The "kind" determines what fits in the ark

In the Fundamentalist, Creationist perspective, the concept of "kind" refers to a distinct grouping of organisms that share a common ancestry and are capable of reproducing and producing fertile offspring among themselves. According to this view, God created various "kinds" of organisms during the six-day creation period as described in the book of Genesis. These "kinds" are considered to be the created forms from which the diversity of life we see today has descended through speciation and adaptation over time.

This is perplexing in light of the inconsistent usage of "kind" found within Scripture. Deuteronomy 14:5, for example, offers the grouping of a "sheep" and "mountain sheep" violating the precise delineation of the term "kind." A similar problem arises when exploring the use of the term "kinds" in Leviticus 11:14-19. This inconsistency of the concept of "kind" becomes increasingly evident through the explicit identification of "several kinds of hawk," "several kinds of heron, hoopoe, and bat," alongside the detailed listing of specific owl types, including the "horned owl, night owl, and barn owl," and so on.

Fundamentalists and Creationists believe the Scriptural reference supporting the concept of "kind" can be found in Genesis 1, where it repeatedly states that God created living creatures "according to their kinds." For instance, in Genesis 1:11-12, it is written: "Then God said, 'Let the land produce vegetation: seed-bearing plants and trees on the land that bear fruit with seed in it, according to their various kinds.' And it was so."

However, the idea of "kind" has led to interpretations and contradictions when attempting to classify and define the exact boundaries of these created groups. The term "kind" in Scripture lacks a precise biological definition, which has led to different interpretations among Creationists regarding its taxonomic implications. Some Creationists propose that "kind" represents a higher taxonomic level than species, while others argue that it corresponds to the species level.

A significant Scriptural reference that showcases the contradiction arises in the account of the Flood and Noah's Ark in Genesis 6 and 7. God instructs Noah to bring two of every "kind" of land-dwelling animal onto the Ark to preserve their lineage during the catastrophic flood. The challenge emerges when attempting to determine the specific number of animals that Noah was required to take, given the ambiguity surrounding the term "kind." If "kind" corresponds to a higher taxonomic level, then Noah would have had to bring significantly fewer animals onto the Ark than if "kind" was interpreted as the species level.

Furthermore, when considering Leviticus 11, which outlines dietary laws and lists various animals, birds, and insects that are considered clean and unclean for consumption, the lack of clear taxonomic categories based on the concept of "kind" becomes evident.

Therefore, the concept of "kind" from a Fundamentalist, Creationist perspective offers a theological framework for understanding the origin and diversity of life as outlined in Scripture. However, its application in specific instances, such as Noah's Ark and Leviticus 11, presents challenges and contradictions due to the lack of precise biological definitions provided within the biblical texts.

9.6 All animals were Herbivores

Creationists who interpret the Genesis 1:29-31 passage in a strict or literal manner argue that before the Flood, all animals were herbivores. The passage states:

"Then God said, 'I give you every seed-bearing plant on the face of the whole earth and every tree that has fruit with seed in it. They will be yours for food. And to all the beasts of the earth and all the birds in the sky and all the creatures that move along the ground—everything that has the breath of life in it—I give every green plant for food.' And it was so."

From a theological perspective, these Creationists believe that this passage presents a picture of the original, harmonious, and peaceful state of nature before the Fall of humankind, where animals were created to live in harmony, not preying on one another. In this view, predation and carnivorous behavior among animals would have emerged after the Fall because of the corruption and brokenness introduced into the world.

From a scientific perspective, the idea that all animals were originally herbivores and became carnivores only after the Fall faces significant challenges. The fossil record, comparative anatomy, and modern scientific understanding of ecosystems and predator-prey relationships all point to the long-standing presence of carnivorous behavior in the animal kingdom.

Fossil evidence shows that predation and carnivores existed for millions of years, long before the emergence of humans. Fossils of predatory animals with specialized teeth and adaptations for hunting have been discovered throughout geological history.

The teeth, jaws, and digestive systems of many animal species are adapted to consume meat. Carnivores typically have sharp teeth for tearing flesh, while herbivores have flat teeth for grinding plant matter. These anatomical features are consistent with the dietary preferences of these animals.

Predation plays a crucial role in maintaining ecological balance and regulating populations of prey species. Removing carnivorous behavior from ecosystems would have significant ecological implications and disrupt the balance of nature.

The claim that all animals were herbivores before the Fall is not supported by scientific evidence. Instead, the scientific understanding of predator-prey relationships and carnivorous adaptations points to the existence of such behavior throughout the history of life on Earth.

The claim that all animals were herbivores before the Flood is primarily rooted in certain theological interpretations of the Genesis account. However, from a scientific perspective, the evidence from fossils, comparative anatomy, and ecological relationships strongly supports the long-standing presence of carnivorous behavior in the animal kingdom.

9.7 Sea Fossils in Mountainous Regions

Fundamentalists and Creationists who interpret the marine fossils found in mountainous regions as evidence of a global flood often base their claims on a literal reading of the biblical account of the Flood found in Genesis 6-9. They believe that the global flood described in the Bible covered the entire planet, and the marine fossils in mountainous areas are seen as remnants of the catastrophic flood event.

From a theological standpoint, these believers argue that accepting a global flood provides evidence for the historicity and accuracy of the biblical narrative. They see the flood as a significant event in human history, illustrating God's judgment on human sinfulness and His providential care for the righteous, as exemplified through Noah and his family.

While marine fossils in mountainous regions may indeed be found at high elevations, the interpretation of these fossils as evidence of a global flood is not supported by mainstream scientific understanding. There are several reasons for and against such a claim:

The presence of marine fossils in mountainous areas can be explained by tectonic processes. Over geological time, Earth's crust experiences uplift and deformation, which can bring ancient marine sediments to higher elevations, forming mountain ranges. Fossils found in these rocks may indicate past marine environments that have been uplifted due to tectonic forces.

The global flood claim is rooted in a literal interpretation of the Bible. For those who hold a strict literalist view of the Bible, the presence of marine fossils in mountainous regions aligns with their understanding of the Flood narrative as a global event.

Modern geology provides robust evidence of the gradual formation of mountains and the movement of tectonic plates over millions of years. The processes of plate tectonics, erosion, and deposition are well-documented and explain the presence of marine fossils in mountainous regions without the need for a global flood.

The global flood claim faces numerous scientific challenges, such as the lack of geological evidence for a global flood event that could have caused such widespread and rapid sedimentation on a global scale. The scientific community has not found compelling evidence of a global flood in its geological record.

The presence of marine fossils in mountainous areas is not limited to a few locations but is a widespread phenomenon observed worldwide. This distribution aligns more with the natural processes of tectonics and geology than with a catastrophic global flood event.

While some fundamentalists may see marine fossils in mountainous regions as evidence of a global flood, the scientific consensus points to alternative explanations. Modern geology and plate tectonics provide more plausible and well-supported reasons for the presence of marine fossils at high elevations, without the need to invoke a worldwide flood event. The claim of a global flood based on marine fossils is primarily rooted in a specific theological interpretation of the Bible rather than being supported by empirical scientific evidence.

9.8 Coexistence of humans and dinosaurs

The notion of humans and dinosaurs coexisting within Earth's history has captivated the imagination of both Creationists and Fundamentalists, offering a unique vantage point that harmonizes scriptural teachings with geological evidence. Through these perspectives, enriched by Scriptural references and geological insights, the potential coexistence of these creatures gains theological and natural significance.

From the Creationist standpoint, the coexistence of humans and dinosaurs is rooted in a literal interpretation of the biblical creation account. Creationists often assert that the universe was created in six literal days, leading to the existence of humans and animals, including dinosaurs, within the same timeframe. While the word "dinosaur" is a relatively recent scientific term, some believe that creatures referred to in Scripture as "behemoth" and "leviathan" (Job 40-41) may describe dinosaurs. Creationists argue that these creatures could have lived alongside humans, as described in Genesis 1:24-31, where all land animals, including dinosaurs, were created on the same day as humans.

Geological evidence can be seen as supportive of this perspective. Fossilized footprints and tracks found in rock formations are often cited as potential evidence of human-dinosaur interaction. Some Creationists point to instances where human-like footprints appear alongside dinosaur tracks in specific geological layers. The presence of soft tissue and DNA fragments in some dinosaur fossils challenges the notion of their extreme antiquity and raises questions about their temporal proximity to humans.

Fundamentalists, meanwhile, uphold the historical reliability of the Bible while acknowledging the possibility of humans and dinosaurs coexisting. They maintain that the Bible provides an accurate account of God's creative work while acknowledging that the text does not provide exhaustive details about all creatures present during that time.

Geological evidence is interpreted through a lens of biblical history, considering the rapid sediment deposition and catastrophic events associated with the global Flood. Fundamentalists suggest that the worldwide deluge could have led to the preservation of both humans and dinosaurs in fossilized forms, with catastrophic burial accounting for the relatively rapid fossilization process.

The coexistence of humans and dinosaurs presents a fascinating perspective that integrates Creationist and Fundamentalist viewpoints. While distinct in approach, both perspectives emphasize the reliability of Scripture and the potential for harmony between geological evidence and the biblical account. Geological formations featuring possible human-dinosaur interactions, along with the preservation of soft tissue in dinosaur fossils, offer intriguing clues to the idea that these magnificent creatures may have walked the Earth alongside humans. Through these perspectives, believers are encouraged to explore the fascinating interplay between faith, science, and the mysteries of creation.

10 The Flood from a Scientific and Theological View

10.1 Likelihood of a Flood

The biblical account of the Flood, as described in the book of Genesis, has been a subject of much debate and scrutiny from both religious and scientific perspectives. From a scientific standpoint, the feasibility of a worldwide flood raising the water level to cover all landmasses on Earth is examined critically. Several legitimate reasons support the scientific view concerning the likelihood of the biblical Flood account.

Firstly, geology and paleontology offer valuable insights into Earth's history and past environmental conditions. The extensive geological record, which spans millions of years, reveals no evidence of a global flood event that inundated the entire planet. Geological formations, such as sediment layers and rock strata, show a gradual accumulation over vast periods, consistent with natural processes like erosion, deposition, and tectonic activity. There is no evidence of a catastrophic flood that would match the biblical description in the geological record.

Secondly, the Earth's ecosystems and biodiversity provide further evidence against a global flood. If the Flood described in the Bible were a reality, it would have caused significant disruption to ecosystems and led to widespread extinctions of plant and animal species. However, the fossil record shows that life on Earth has undergone gradual changes and transitions over time, without sudden mass extinctions due to a global flood.

Furthermore, the logistics and practicalities of housing and preserving millions of species on a wooden ark raise considerable challenges. Building an ark of the dimensions described in the Bible that could accommodate all known species, along with the necessary provisions for their survival, presents numerous difficulties. Additionally, the ecological impact of releasing such a large number of animals back into the wild after the floodwaters receded would have caused further disruptions to ecosystems.

Modern scientific understanding of hydrology[xxxii] and rainfall patterns also challenges the feasibility of a global flood event. The amount of water required to cover all landmasses on Earth to the extent described in the Bible exceeds the capacity of the Earth's water reservoirs[xxxiii], including oceans, rivers, and groundwater. The evaporation, condensation, and precipitation cycles that govern the Earth's water balance would not permit such a sudden and massive increase in global water levels.

Finally, the cultural and literary context of the biblical account should be considered. Flood stories are not unique to the Bible but are found in various ancient civilizations[xxxiv] worldwide, indicating that they might have been symbolic or mythological narratives shared by different cultures to convey moral or religious teachings. The biblical Flood account, in this light, could be interpreted as a theological and symbolic story rather than a literal historical event.

The scientific perspective raises significant challenges to the likelihood of the biblical account of the Flood. Geology, paleontology, biology, hydrology, and practical considerations all contribute to a comprehensive evaluation that casts doubt on the feasibility of a worldwide flood event. While the biblical narrative holds religious and theological significance, approaching it from a scientific standpoint provides a more nuanced understanding of the natural processes that have shaped Earth's history and the development of life on our planet.

10.2 Ark construction issues

From a scientific perspective:

The concept of Noah and his seven relatives being able to harvest the resources for an ark of such immense size and scale in biblical times presents numerous difficulties from a scientific standpoint. The construction of an ark with the dimensions described in the Bible would indeed require an enormous amount of lumber, approximately 3.1 million board feet[lxxxv], which is an incredibly massive undertaking.

1. **Technological limitations:** During biblical times, around 4,000 to 5,000 years ago, human civilizations lacked advanced tools and machinery that would have been necessary for such large-scale construction. The absence of heavy machinery, cranes, and modern transportation methods would have made it nearly impossible to fell, process, and transport such a vast amount of lumber.

2. **Feasibility of resources:** The sheer amount of lumber required to build the ark, approximately 3.1 million board feet, is a considerable challenge. According to the Creation Museum, the lumber required to build the ark would require 3.1 million board feet, (i.e., 12" x 12" x 1"). To put that in perspective, it would be enough lumber to stretch from Kentucky to New York as the crow flies.

3. **Machinery and tools required:** During biblical times, the available technology and tools were not sufficient for

such large-scale logging and processing of wood. The logistics of obtaining and transporting such a vast quantity of lumber in the absence of modern machinery and transportation methods are difficult to imagine.

4. **Time constraints:** According to the biblical account, Noah and his family had a limited timeframe of roughly 75 years to complete the construction of the ark (Genesis 6:3). This is a relatively short span, given the scale of the project and the limited number of workers available. The sheer volume of lumber required to build the ark in this time frame seems highly improbable.

5. **Sourcing materials:** The biblical account places Noah and his family in the region of Mesopotamia. Acquiring such a vast amount of lumber from the available local resources in that region would have been extremely challenging. Forests capable of supplying the required lumber were not present in the region[lxxxvi], which raises questions about how they could have obtained such a large quantity of wood.

6. **Design and engineering challenges:** Building a seaworthy vessel of that size presents significant engineering challenges. The biblical dimensions of the ark are approximately 510 feet long, 85 feet wide, and 51 feet high (Genesis 6:15). Constructing a wooden ship of such dimensions without modern engineering knowledge would have resulted in structural issues, making it difficult to withstand the forces of the ocean.

From a theological perspective:

While the story of Noah and the Ark is considered a central narrative in Abrahamic religions and holds deep theological significance, the implausibility of building such an ark is often approached in different ways:

1. **Divine intervention:** Many adherents of the biblical account see the construction of the Ark as a miracle orchestrated by God. From this perspective, God's involvement ensured that Noah and his family were able to accomplish the task despite the apparent difficulties. The only problem with this is that there is no Scriptural evidence to support such a claim.

2. **Symbolic interpretation:** Some theologians and scholars interpret the story of Noah and the Ark as a symbolic narrative rather than a literal historical event. They view it as a story that conveys moral and spiritual lessons, rather than an accurate account of a worldwide flood and an enormous ark.

3. **Allegorical meaning:** From a theological perspective, the focus might shift from the practicality of building such an ark to the theological truths embedded in the story, such as the themes of faith, obedience, and divine mercy.

Ultimately, the story of Noah and the Ark, like many biblical narratives, has been a subject of interpretation and debate among scholars and believers for centuries. The focus on the plausibility of its construction varies based on one's approach to religious texts and personal beliefs.

The concept of Noah and his family harvesting the resources to build the ark, as described in the biblical account, presents significant difficulties from both scientific and theological perspectives. While the story carries deep theological significance and has been central to Abrahamic faiths for centuries, scholars and believers continue to interpret it in various ways, often focusing on its symbolic and allegorical meanings rather than its literal feasibility.

10.3 Drinking Water on the Ark

The account of Noah and the ark in Genesis 8:3, where rain ceased to fall from heaven, raises questions about how Noah and the inhabitants of the ark obtained drinking water during this extended period. From a scientific perspective, understanding this scenario involves considering hydrological and climatic factors that could have facilitated the collection and availability of water for consumption.

The cessation of rainfall and the subsequent availability of water for drinking in the ark could be attributed to various natural processes. One possibility is that after the initial period of heavy rainfall that caused the floodwaters, the climate and atmospheric conditions shifted, leading to a reduction in precipitation. This shift might have been influenced by factors such as changing weather patterns, atmospheric pressure systems, or the cooling of ocean surfaces that can impact the formation of rain clouds.

Another process that could have contributed to the availability of drinking water is the condensation of water vapor in the atmosphere. During periods of humidity or temperature changes, water vapor in the air can condense into droplets. These droplets can accumulate on surfaces and be collected as liquid water. If the atmosphere within and around the ark became humid due to the large amount of water present, condensation could have occurred, resulting in the formation of water droplets that could be collected and utilized for drinking.

In the realm of scientific possibility, such processes align with natural mechanisms of water collection and condensation. These processes could have been responsible for providing the inhabitants of the ark with a continuous supply of drinking water when rain ceased to fall. While the specific conditions and factors at play are subject to scientific investigation and speculation, the potential for such processes to occur underlines the remarkable adaptability of the natural world.

Biblical examples of God's provision in challenging circumstances resonate with the idea of water collection through natural processes. In Exodus 16:13-15, the Israelites in the wilderness are provided with manna from heaven. Similarly, God's provision of water from a rock in Exodus 17:6 showcases His ability to provide sustenance through unconventional means. These examples reflect the theme of divine care and intervention, which could find resonance in the narrative of Noah's Ark as well.

The cessation of rain in Genesis 8:3 and the availability of drinking water for Noah and the inhabitants of the ark can be considered within the framework of natural processes such as changing climatic conditions and atmospheric water vapor condensation. These processes, while scientifically plausible, highlight the intricate interactions of the natural world. Biblical examples of divine provision further underscore the concept of God's care even in the face of challenging circumstances.

10.4 Illumination in the lower decks of the ark

The depiction of the lower deck's illumination on Noah's Ark, as portrayed in the Book of Genesis, raises numerous challenges. The Genesis account, while a foundational narrative within the Judeo-Christian tradition, presents several inconsistencies and implausible aspects when it comes to the technological feasibility of constructing a massive vessel that housed pairs of every living creature. In the absence of detailed technical specifications and considering the rudimentary technological capabilities of the time, the notion of illuminating the lower deck becomes a contentious point.

Genesis 6:14-16 outlines the instructions given to Noah for constructing the ark, including its dimensions and layout. However, the text remains conspicuously silent on matters related to lighting or illumination within the ark. The Hebrew word "e'thbe[lxxxvii], הַ‍תֵּ‍בָ‍ה " translated as "window" or "roof" in some versions, offers limited insight into the actual mechanics of how light would have been facilitated. This term's ambiguity further complicates attempts to establish a concrete understanding of how illumination was achieved on the lower deck.

The available technology and materials during Noah's time present significant obstacles to achieving effective illumination on the lower deck of the ark. The Genesis account places the construction of the ark around 4,000 to 5,000 years ago, a period characterized by limited tools, resources, and engineering knowledge. The use of glass or advanced translucent materials, which would be necessary to create effective windows or skylights, was likely beyond the technological capabilities of that era.

Moreover, the dimensions of the ark as described in Genesis 6:15, (300 cubits in length, 50 cubits in width, and 30 cubits in height), further exacerbate the illumination challenge. The vast size of the ark, along with the absence of architectural techniques for structurally sound windows or openings, raises questions about the plausibility of uniformly distributing natural light throughout the lower deck.

In the absence of detailed architectural plans or archaeological evidence, skeptics contend that the illumination of the lower deck remains an implausible aspect of the Noah's Ark narrative. Despite lack of Scriptural support to indicate divine illumination, the Genesis account itself emphasizes the supernatural aspects of the story, suggesting divine intervention beyond the scope of human technological capabilities. As such, the focus on how the lower deck was illuminated can be seen as a secondary concern, overshadowed by the broader theological themes and moral lessons the narrative seeks to convey.

The skepticism surrounding the illumination of the lower deck of Noah's Ark stems from the technological limitations of the time, the absence of concrete architectural details in the Genesis account, and the overarching focus on theological and moral themes. While the narrative itself does not delve into the intricacies of illumination, it catalyzes discussions on the intersections of faith, science, and the interpretation of ancient texts.

10.5 How did the lower deck stay dry?

There are significant challenges in understanding how the lower deck of such a vessel as massive as Noah's Ark could remain dry throughout a worldwide flood. The account, as depicted in the Book of Genesis, presents numerous inconsistencies and implausible aspects when scrutinized within the context of the available technology and engineering knowledge during the time the ark was purportedly constructed. Examining the dimensions of the ark, construction methods, and the lack of sophisticated drainage systems, it becomes increasingly difficult to reconcile the idea that the lower deck could have remained dry during the flood event.

Genesis 6:14-16 provides instructions for building the ark, including its dimensions and layout. However, the text does not offer explicit details about waterproofing techniques or the design features necessary to prevent water ingress into the lower deck. The omission of such technical aspects raises skepticism about the practical feasibility of constructing a vessel of such magnitude that could effectively keep water out.

The biblical chronology places the construction and flood events around 4,000 to 5,000 years ago, an era marked by limited technology, basic construction tools, and a lack of advanced materials. The ark's massive dimensions, as specified in Genesis 6:15, further complicates the challenge of waterproofing. With a length of 300 cubits, a width of 50 cubits, and a height of 30 cubits, the vast interior space presents difficulties in maintaining structural integrity, especially without the use of modern construction techniques and waterproofing materials.

In addition to these challenges, the absence of detailed blueprints or archaeological evidence leaves significant gaps in our understanding of the ark's construction and waterproofing methods. The skeptics argue that the narrative in Genesis emphasizes divine intervention and miraculous elements, which some interpret as indications that the story is meant to convey theological and moral lessons rather than providing a practical blueprint for shipbuilding.

Furthermore, the ark's purpose as a vessel to house a diverse array of animals for an extended period casts doubt on its functionality as a seaworthy structure. The challenges of feeding, waste disposal, and ventilation for such a diverse population within a wooden structure add complexities that the Genesis narrative does not explicitly address.

The notion of the lower deck of Noah's a Ark remaining dry during a worldwide flood poses substantial challenges. The absence of detailed architectural and waterproofing specifications, the technological constraints of the time, and the practicalities of maintaining such a massive wooden vessel all contribute to skepticism about the narrative's feasibility. This perspective underscores the need to interpret ancient texts within their cultural and historical contexts while also acknowledging the ongoing dialogue between faith, science, and critical analysis.

10.6 The Wyoming schooner

The Flood account in the Book of Genesis describes the construction of an immense wooden vessel, commonly known as Noah's Ark, designed to preserve various living creatures during a global deluge. It is important to scientifically examine the plausibility of the ark as an ocean-worthy vessel, drawing comparisons with the Wyoming[lxxxviii] schooner built in 1909, the longest wooden ship ever constructed by skilled shipbuilders, which measured 450 feet in length. By considering the biblical dimensions of the ark and its ocean-worthiness, this analysis will explore the challenges and limitations inherent in constructing such a massive wooden structure for seafaring purposes.

According to Genesis 6:14-16, God instructs Noah to build an ark with the following dimensions: "Make yourself an ark of gopher wood. Make rooms in the ark and cover it inside and out with pitch. This is how you are to make it: the length of the ark 300 cubits, its breadth 50 cubits, and its height 30 cubits."

Given that the length of the cubit[lxxxix] was measured from the elbow to the tip of the middle finger, it is not surprising that Sumerians, Egyptians and Israelites had different dimensions.

Consequently, the length of the cubit in the Bible varies in different sources ranging[xc] from 18 inches to 25 inches. So, the length of the Ark would have been between 450 and 625 feet, a dimension strikingly similar and perhaps larger than the length of the Wyoming schooner. That said, the Wyoming Schooner offers a fair comparison with Noah's Ark.

The Wyoming schooner was a colossal wooden ship constructed in the late 19th century, measuring 450 feet in length. This vessel holds the distinction of being the longest wooden ship ever built by skilled craftsmen. Wyoming was designed primarily for carrying cargo, particularly coal, across the Atlantic Ocean. Although it was a technological marvel of its time, the Wyoming schooner encountered numerous challenges and eventually faced operational issues due to its immense size.

The construction of a wooden vessel as long as 450 feet presents significant engineering challenges. Wooden ships of such dimensions, like the Wyoming schooner, are prone to structural weaknesses and inherent instability. The weight distribution, the sheer size of the hull, and the forces experienced during ocean travel all contribute to the implausibility of the ark as a seaworthy vessel.

The Wyoming schooner experienced difficulties in maintaining stability due to its length-to-beam ratio[xci]. The ark, with its length-to-beam ratio of approximately 6:1, (i.e., 30 to 5 to 3), would face even greater challenges in staying upright in turbulent waters. The ark's capacity to withstand wave forces, weather storms, and provide a steady platform for the vast number of living creatures it was meant to carry appears highly improbable.

The ark was described as being constructed from "gopher wood," a term whose meaning remains unclear. However, such a wooden material would not possess the structural strength and durability necessary for a vessel of such dimensions. The challenges of securing and waterproofing a wooden vessel of this scale further diminish the ark's feasibility as an ocean-worthy ship.

Upon a scholarly scientific evaluation, it becomes evident that the ark, as described in the Genesis Flood account, would face considerable implausibility as an ocean-worthy vessel, given its dimensions and the known limitations of constructing and navigating wooden ships of such colossal size. While the story of Noah's Ark holds profound spiritual significance for various religious traditions, interpreting the narrative as a historically literal description of an ocean-faring vessel would require suspension of scientific scrutiny. Instead, the account may be better understood as an allegorical representation of faith, divine providence, and the preservation of life in the face of cataclysmic events.

10.7 Likelihood of gathering the animals

The account of Noah's Ark, as described in the Book of Genesis, has long been a subject of fascination, debate, and inquiry. One of the key challenges that arise from this narrative is the feasibility of gathering, housing, and feeding a vast assortment of animals within the confines of the ark. From a common-sense and reason-based perspective, several practical considerations emerge that cast doubt on the literal interpretation of this aspect of the story.

Firstly, the sheer diversity and number of species on Earth present a significant logistical challenge. Genesis 6:21-23 indicates that "Every living thing that moved on land perished—

birds, livestock, wild animals, all the creatures that swarm over the earth, and all mankind. Everything on dry land that had the breath of life in its nostrils died. Every living thing on the face of the earth was wiped out; people and animals and the creatures that move along the ground and the birds were wiped from the earth." The verses unambiguously indicate that everything that was not on the Ark perished, that would include insects and plants, unless, of course, they could survive after being submerged for a year in salt water.

Estimates place the number of extant species at 8.75 million[xcii], encompassing a wide range of dietary requirements, environmental conditions, and sizes. Housing and providing sustenance for such an array of creatures within a single vessel would require an immense amount of space, resources, and careful planning. Moreover, many species have specific habitats, food sources, and ecological relationships that would be difficult to replicate on the ark. For instance, carnivores might require prey animals to sustain themselves, creating an additional need for space and provisioning.

Secondly, the matter of the ark's structural integrity and size poses further questions. The biblical description of the ark's dimensions as 300 cubits in length, 50 cubits in width, and 30 cubits in height suggests a vessel of substantial proportions. However, even with these dimensions, the challenges of accommodating such a vast assortment of animals remain formidable. The preservation of distinct habitats, ventilation, waste management, and temperature control for creatures originating from various ecosystems would require sophisticated engineering solutions that surpass the technological capabilities of the time.

Lastly, the logistics of gathering animals from across the globe raise practical difficulties. The story of the ark implies the collection of animals from different continents and ecosystems, which would involve traversing vast distances and overcoming geographical barriers. Additionally, many species have specific dietary needs and are dependent on particular foods that might not be readily available on the ark. Ensuring an adequate supply of appropriate sustenance for each species would be a daunting task.

When examining the likelihood of Noah and his family gathering, housing, and feeding all the animals in the ark, common sense and reason raise substantial challenges. The immense diversity of species, the complex requirements of different ecosystems, the practicalities of structural design and engineering, and the difficulties of procuring and storing sufficient quantities of food all contribute to a narrative that is difficult to reconcile with scientific understanding and practical realities. As such, interpretations of the Noah's Ark story often involve symbolic, allegorical, or theological interpretations that go beyond a strictly literal reading.

10.8 From "kind" to species

Remember that a critical factor determining how many animals will fit on the ark hinges on the Fundamentalist and Creationist definition of "kind". So much easier to bring a thousand animals than 8.75 million species.

Another constraint was having food for the animals that Noah took with him. This, of course, was much easier to address given the Fundamentalist and Creationist notion that at the time of the Flood, all animals were herbivores. As I mentioned earlier, there is adequate evidence to suggest otherwise.

Adherents of the Creationist and Fundamentalist belief system assert that the Great Flood occurred approximately 4,300 years ago and maintain that only 1,000 distinct "kinds" of organisms were necessitated to be accommodated on Noah's Ark. In contrast, modern biological assessments, adopting a highly conservative approach, propose that the Earth presently harbors around 8.75 million distinct species comprising animals, birds, insects, and fish.

This delineation implies that the discrepancy between the two estimates, encompassing 8.75 million species (8.75 million minus 1,000 "kinds"), multiplied by the span of 4,300 years and the average of 365.25 days per year (yielding 1,570,575), would suggest the emergence of over 5 novel species daily (8,749,000 / 1,570,575 = 5.6). It is nearly incomprehensible to think that each day 5.6 new species would come into existence.

The claim that all species came from "kinds" would lead to improbable outcomes. In the case of dinosaurs, for example, a 5.6 new species would have had to arise *each day* to account for the diversity of observed dinosaur skeletons. In such a scenario, it would have been possible for a Stegosaurus to give birth to a Tyrannosaurus Rex. In turn, a Tyrannosaurus Rex would give birth to a Triceratops, and so on. To me, such a claim sounds utterly preposterous. Also, consider that within 4,300 years those new dinosaurs would somehow perish and be buried in layers of rock.

To offer an example a little more familiar with our experience with dogs, it would be the same as a Labrador Retriever producing a litter containing a German Shepherd. The German Shepherd then giving birth to an English Bulldog. The English Bulldog giving birth to a Poodle, Rottweiler, and so on. To go from one thousand "kinds" to the diversification of species 8.75 million species, (animals, birds, insects, fish), 5.6 new species each day would be a common occurrence. Not only is there a lack of observational evidence, but the probability of such an occurrence violates common sense and logic. To the best of my knowledge, this is not the way things work. Again, keep in mind that 8.75 million species is a very low estimate. As this number increases, the situation becomes more untenable.

Such a rapid diversification of life forms, as implied by this calculation, stands in stark contrast to the gradual pace of species evolution and speciation observed through empirical evidence and well-established scientific principles. Moreover, the fossil record and extensive studies of biodiversity reveal a far more gradual and incremental process of species emergence, spanning over millions of years, which aligns with the framework of modern evolutionary theory.

Considering this stark incongruity, scholars and scientists question the feasibility of reconciling the Fundamentalist and Creationist chronology with the broader understanding of biological evolution and the complexities involved in the origination and diversification of life on Earth. The apparent discrepancy underscores the importance of considering diverse perspectives and employing rigorous scientific methodologies to gain a comprehensive understanding of the natural world and its evolutionary history.

10.9 Dinosaurs and humans did not coexist

The notion of humans and dinosaurs coexisting in the same period, as often depicted in popular culture, lacks empirical support when scrutinized from a scientific standpoint. There are several reasons why evidence suggests that humans and dinosaurs did not coexist, reinforcing the view that these two groups of organisms occupied different epochs in Earth's history.

One of the most significant pieces of evidence is the fossil record itself. Dinosaurs, which went extinct around 65 million years ago during the Cretaceous-Paleogene[xciii] (K-Pg) extinction event, have been extensively studied and documented through their fossil remains. In contrast, the earliest undisputed evidence of anatomically modern humans dates back only around 230,000 years[xciv]. The vast temporal gap between the extinction of dinosaurs and the emergence of humans precludes the possibility of direct interaction between the two groups.

Furthermore, the geological time scale, established through radiometric dating and stratigraphic analysis, provides a robust framework for understanding Earth's history. Dinosaurs inhabited the Mesozoic Era[xcv], which spanned from approximately 252 to 66 million years ago, while humans belong to the Quaternary Period[xcvi], starting around 2.6 million years ago. The clear distinction in periods, as supported by precise dating methods, reinforces the idea that humans and dinosaurs did not coexist.

The anatomical and ecological differences between humans and dinosaurs also underscore their distinct epochs. Dinosaurs were a diverse group of reptiles adapted to various ecological niches, ranging from small herbivores to massive predators. Humans, on the other hand, belong to the lineage of primates and possess distinct features such as an upright posture, bipedal locomotion, and advanced cognitive abilities. The unique characteristics of dinosaurs and humans indicate separate evolutionary trajectories over millions of years.

Additionally, the absence of any direct physical evidence, such as dinosaur depictions in ancient art or human artifacts in dinosaur-bearing sediment layers, further supports the idea of their non-coexistence. Despite numerous ancient cultures leaving behind intricate art and artifacts, there is no credible evidence suggesting that humans encountered or interacted with dinosaurs.

The age of various geological formations also corroborates the idea of temporal separation between humans and dinosaurs. While dinosaur fossils are found in sediment layers from the Mesozoic Era, human fossils and artifacts are found in much younger layers, reflecting the distinct periods of their existence.

The scientific perspective presents a strong case against the coexistence of humans and dinosaurs. The substantial temporal gap revealed by the fossil record, the geological time scale, and precise dating methods firmly place dinosaurs and humans in separate eras of Earth's history. The anatomical and ecological distinctions between the two groups, along with the absence of direct evidence of interaction, provide further support for the legitimate view that humans and dinosaurs did not coexist.

10.10 Stratification of fossils in rock

The discovery of fossils in lower strata of rock provides compelling evidence that conflicts with the depiction of a global flood as described in the Genesis flood account. From a scientific perspective, the distribution of fossils and the layers in which they are found present significant challenges to the notion of a catastrophic flood inundating the entire planet. Several key reasons contribute to this conflict.

Stratigraphy[xcvii], the study of rock layers and their chronological sequence offers valuable insights into Earth's history. Fossils found in lower strata of rock, such as those from the Cambrian Explosion[xcviii] around 541 million years ago, display an array of complex and diverse organisms. This biological diversity contradicts the expectations of a global flood, which would be expected to result in a chaotic mixing of species throughout the sediment layers. Instead, the fossil record demonstrates a clear order of species appearing over time, suggesting gradual evolution rather than a sudden catastrophic event.

Moreover, the principles of relative dating and superposition provide a framework for understanding the arrangement of rock layers and fossils. The Law of Superposition[xcix] states that in undisturbed layers of rock, younger strata are found above older ones. This concept aligns with the observed pattern of fossils becoming more complex as we move upwards through the rock layers. For instance, the trilobites found in the Cambrian layers are more primitive than the mammals found in higher, more recent layers. This sequential arrangement of fossils is inconsistent with a global flood that would be expected to jumble and mix organisms from various periods.

Additionally, the presence of localized fossils, such as those found exclusively in specific regions, also contradicts the notion of a worldwide flood. Fossilized remains of animals and plants, such as marsupials and eucalyptus trees, are found primarily in Australia, indicating regional habitats and ecosystems. These regional distributions are not compatible with the idea of a flood that would uniformly distribute species across the globe.

The fossil record also reveals patterns of extinction and survival that challenge the flood hypothesis. The K-Pg extinction event[c] around 65 million years ago wiped out the non-avian dinosaurs but allowed the rise of mammals and birds. If a global flood occurred, one would expect to find mixed and jumbled remains of these different groups. However, the fossil record demonstrates clear boundaries between extinct and surviving species, consistent with gradual processes of evolution and natural selection rather than a catastrophic flood event.

The distribution of fossils in lower strata of rock provides substantial evidence that conflicts with the Genesis flood account. Stratigraphy, relative dating principles, localized fossils, and patterns of extinction all point to a gradual and intricate history of life on Earth, rather than the rapid and catastrophic events associated with a global flood. The scientific perspective on the fossil record supports a nuanced understanding of Earth's history, characterized by the gradual emergence and evolution of diverse species over vast periods.

11 Insights into the Genesis Flood

11.1 Other Ancient Flood Accounts

The Epic of Gilgamesh[ci] and the Genesis flood narrative share similarities, and the former has been considered by some scholars as supporting evidence of the latter. The Epic of Gilgamesh is an ancient Mesopotamian epic poem from the Sumerian[cii] and Akkadian[ciii] civilizations, dating back to around 2100 BCE for the earliest versions. It predates the written accounts of the Genesis flood, which are part of the Hebrew Bible, by several centuries.

Similarities between the two tales include:

The Flood Story: Both epics contain an account of a catastrophic flood that covers the entire world. In both narratives, the protagonist is warned by a god (Ea in the Epic of Gilgamesh and Yahweh in Genesis) about the impending flood and instructed to build a vessel to save themselves, their family, and various animals.

The Ark or Boat: In both tales, the protagonist constructs a boat to escape the flood and save living creatures. The dimensions of the vessels are also mentioned in both stories.

Release of Birds: After the flood subsides, both protagonists release birds (a dove and a raven) to determine if the waters have receded sufficiently.

Divine Wrath and Preservation of Righteous: In both stories, the flood is seen because of divine anger and judgment. The protagonist, who is considered righteous, is spared from the devastation.

Despite these similarities, there are also significant differences between the two accounts. For example, in the Epic of Gilgamesh, the flood is a result of the gods' decision to eliminate humankind due to their noise and overpopulation, while in the Genesis flood, it is attributed to the wickedness of humanity.

The time difference between the two tales is substantial. As mentioned earlier, the earliest versions of the Epic of Gilgamesh date back to around 2100 BCE, making it one of the oldest surviving literary works. On the other hand, the written accounts of the Genesis flood are believed to have been compiled much later, likely between the 6th and 5th centuries BCE, during the Babylonian exile.

The prevailing scholarly consensus is that the Epic of Gilgamesh is an older narrative, and the similarities between the two stories are due to cultural diffusion and the shared traditions between the ancient civilizations of Mesopotamia and the Israelites. The Genesis flood narrative likely drew upon and adapted existing flood stories in the region, incorporating them into the broader Hebrew religious and cultural context.

The Epic of Gilgamesh can be seen as supporting evidence of flood narratives in ancient civilizations, including the Genesis flood. However, the Genesis flood narrative is distinct in its theological and religious context and was compiled much later than the Epic of Gilgamesh.

11.2 Which flood came first?

From a standpoint of logic and historical chronology, if the Epic of Gilgamesh predates the Genesis flood account, it is not feasible to assume that the Genesis flood preceded the flood recorded in the Epic of Gilgamesh. The order of the written texts indicates the sequence of their creation, but it does not imply that the events described in the later text necessarily occurred before the events in the earlier text.

The chronological order of the texts does not dictate the chronological order of the events they describe. The Epic of Gilgamesh may have been written before the Genesis flood account, but that does not mean the flood events in the Epic of Gilgamesh happened before the flood events described in Genesis.

The flood accounts in both epics are believed to have originated from older oral traditions that predate the written versions. The Epic of Gilgamesh may have preserved an older flood story that was later adapted and incorporated into the Genesis flood narrative. The similarities between the two accounts, as well as other flood myths from various ancient cultures, suggest a common cultural heritage and shared stories of catastrophic floods.

It is essential to distinguish between the literary order of the texts and the historical order of the events they describe. While the Epic of Gilgamesh is an earlier written text, it doesn't necessarily indicate the occurrence of the flood events described in the epic before the flood events in the Genesis account. The precise historical order of events is challenging to establish for ancient narratives, especially when they are part of oral traditions passed down through generations before being written down.

11.3 Could the Black Sea Deluge explain the Genesis Flood?

The Black Sea Deluge Hypothesis[civ] has received significant attention among geologists and archaeologists as a potential key to understanding past catastrophic flooding events in the

Black Sea region. Proposed in the late 1990s, this hypothesis posits that a substantial rise in sea levels led to the flooding of the Black Sea basin during the early Holocene period[cv]. It is important to explore the Black Sea Deluge Hypothesis and examine how it can offer insights into the Genesis Flood account from the Book of Genesis.

According to the Black Sea Deluge Hypothesis, around 7,500 years ago, during the Mesolithic era[cvi], the Mediterranean Sea experienced a significant rise in sea level. As glacial ice melted and oceanic levels increased, the rising water eventually breached the natural land barrier between the Mediterranean and the Black Sea. This allowed a catastrophic influx of seawater into the previously freshwater Black Sea basin. The sudden and massive flooding event caused a dramatic increase in water levels, profoundly altering the local landscape and affecting human populations inhabiting the region.

The Black Sea Deluge Hypothesis holds intriguing parallels with the Genesis Flood account found in the Bible. Genesis 7:11 states, "In the six hundredth year of Noah's life, in the second month, on the seventeenth day of the month, on that day all the fountains of the great deep burst forth, and the windows of the heavens were opened." This biblical passage describes a global flood triggered by an outpouring of water from both the sky and the depths of the Earth. While the Black Sea Deluge was a regional event, its catastrophic nature aligns with the dramatic flood described in the Genesis narrative.

Genesis 7:20 mentions, "The waters prevailed fifteen cubits upward, and the mountains were covered." This scriptural reference bears similarity to the rapid increase in water levels during the Black Sea Deluge, where the water is estimated to have risen several meters per day until it reached its current level. Additionally, Genesis 7:19 states, "And the waters prevailed so mightily on the earth that all the high mountains under the whole heaven were covered." The Black Sea Deluge's impact on the surrounding landscape would have been similarly vast and transformative.

Numerous lines of evidence support the Black Sea Deluge Hypothesis. Archaeological excavations have revealed submerged settlements and ancient artifacts on the Black Sea's seabed, indicating the presence of human habitation before the deluge. Sediment cores collected from the seabed contain layers indicative of a sudden and massive inflow of seawater, consistent with a catastrophic flood event. Additionally, geological studies have identified a paleo shoreline at a lower elevation, indicating the Black Sea's former freshwater status before the deluge breached the natural barrier.

The Black Sea Deluge Hypothesis provides a compelling regional context for the Genesis Flood account. By recognizing that ancient cultures living in the Mesopotamian region might have experienced a catastrophic flood event, we can better understand how such events could have shaped collective memory and influenced the narrative found in Genesis. It allows us to view the biblical flood account through a historical lens, acknowledging the potential basis of real events while also appreciating its spiritual significance.

The Black Sea Deluge Hypothesis offers valuable insights into ancient flooding events and their potential connections to cultural narratives such as the Genesis Flood account. By examining geological evidence and Scriptural references, we find compelling parallels between the regional deluge in the Black Sea basin and the biblical global flood. This scholarly exploration deepens our understanding of historical cataclysms and how they may have inspired enduring cultural and religious accounts.

11.4 Occam's Razor

Occam's Razor[cvii], also known as the law of parsimony, is a fundamental principle in scientific reasoning and philosophy that advocates for simplicity as a guiding criterion for selecting between competing explanations or hypotheses. Named after the 14th-century philosopher and theologian William of Ockham, this principle suggests that, all else being equal, the simplest explanation that accounts for the available evidence is most likely to be correct. Occam's Razor serves as a heuristic tool to guide researchers in making informed decisions when faced with multiple hypotheses, aiming to avoid unnecessary complexity and speculative elements in their conclusions.

The principle of Occam's Razor can be understood as an extension of the broader philosophical principle known as the "principle of economy" or "principle of simplicity." This principle asserts that unnecessary assumptions or entities should not be postulated, and explanations should not be made more complicated than necessary. In the context of scientific investigation, this translates to selecting the hypothesis that requires the fewest assumptions or entities to account for the observed phenomena.

One illustrative example of Occam's Razor can be found in the realm of astronomy. When Johannes Kepler proposed his laws of planetary motion in the 17th century, they replaced the complex, epicyclic models that were used to describe planetary orbits. Kepler's laws[cviii], which describe elliptical orbits and the relationship between a planet's distance from the sun and its orbital period, were simpler and more elegant than the convoluted models that preceded them. Kepler's application of Occam's Razor favored simplicity over the unnecessary complexity inherent in the previous models.

Another application can be seen in the field of biology, particularly in discussions about the origin of life. In the search for the origin of complex biochemical molecules, such as proteins and DNA, scientists often encounter hypotheses that involve complex and unlikely scenarios. However, Occam's Razor prompts researchers to consider simpler explanations, such as the possibility that these molecules emerged through basic chemical processes under favorable conditions. This principle encourages researchers to avoid invoking elaborate and speculative mechanisms when simpler explanations are available.

Occam's Razor, while a powerful tool in scientific reasoning, is not a strict rule but rather a guiding principle. It does not dictate that the simplest explanation is always correct, but rather suggests that, given equal explanatory power, the simpler explanation is more likely to be accurate. The principle encourages researchers to balance the quest for understanding with the avoidance of unnecessary complexity, ultimately enhancing the quality of scientific explanations and theories.

11.5 Using Occam's Razor regarding the flood

The application of Occam's Razor to the Flood account in Genesis, as compared with the Black Sea Deluge Hypothesis, offers a fascinating exploration of the intersection between theology and science. Occam's Razor, advocating for simplicity in explaining phenomena, prompts a reevaluation of the global flood narrative considering scientific hypotheses. The Black Sea Deluge Hypothesis proposes that the Flood account may find its origins in the catastrophic flooding of the ancient Black Sea basin due to rising sea levels at the end of the last ice age. This comparative analysis encompasses both the biblical narrative and a cultural counterpart, The Epic of Gilgamesh, contributing to a comprehensive understanding of the challenges and resolutions arising from these interpretations.

From a theological perspective, the application of Occam's Razor to the Flood narrative guides theologians to reconsider the universal scope of the flood event. The traditional understanding of a global flood, as depicted in Genesis, raises intricate theological issues, including the preservation of diverse species and the logistics of such an event. The Black Sea Deluge Hypothesis proposes a more localized flood, providing a simpler explanation for these challenges. This approach also considers The Epic of Gilgamesh, a parallel flood narrative that predates the biblical account, suggesting that the flood event might have been a cultural memory transformed into a divine narrative across various traditions.

The application of Occam's Razor is particularly relevant in overcoming obstacles presented by the geological evidence. While a global flood would leave profound geological traces, the absence of such evidence has posed difficulties for a literal interpretation of the biblical narrative. The Black Sea Deluge Hypothesis, grounded in observable sea-level rise and geological shifts, offers a more scientifically plausible explanation for a localized flood event. This hypothesis also aligns with The Epic of Gilgamesh, wherein a local flood serves as a pivotal event within the narrative. The simplicity of the Black Sea Deluge Hypothesis addresses the lack of global geological evidence and provides a pathway for reconciling the biblical account with scientific findings.

Furthermore, the application of Occam's Razor helps navigate the theological complexities associated with divine intervention. By considering a localized flood, the theological challenge of explaining how all of Earth's species could fit onto Noah's Ark becomes more manageable. Occam's Razor encourages theologians to favor an explanation that requires fewer assumptions and resolves some of the logistical issues. The Black Sea Deluge Hypothesis and the parallel narrative in The Epic of Gilgamesh offer insights into the fusion of cultural memory and divine narratives, shedding light on how shared events can shape religious traditions.

The application of Occam's Razor to the Flood account in Genesis and the Black Sea Deluge Hypothesis provides a thought-provoking framework for reconciling theology and science. This principle prompts a reassessment of the global flood narrative and encourages an exploration of localized events that might have informed the biblical account. By considering scientific evidence, geological data, and cultural parallels like The Epic of Gilgamesh, scholars engage in an interdisciplinary dialogue that enriches our understanding of ancient narratives. This approach showcases how Occam's Razor serves as a bridge between complex theological considerations and empirically observed phenomena, ultimately fostering a more comprehensive and informed discourse on the intricacies of flood narratives.

12 Open Questions in Genesis

12.1 What do we know about Noah?

Noah's character, as depicted in the Scriptures, is a fascinating study of faith, obedience, and human limitations. The scriptural verses present a detailed portrayal of his strengths, weaknesses, and profession, shedding light on the complexities of his character.

Noah's most evident strength lies in his unwavering faith and righteousness. In Genesis 6:9, he is described as a "righteous man, blameless among the people of his time, and he walked faithfully with God." This unyielding devotion to God sets him apart as a righteous figure amidst a corrupt and wicked generation.

Another strength of Noah is his obedience to God's commands. When God revealed His plan to bring a flood to cleanse the Earth, Noah was chosen to build an Ark to save himself, his family, and representatives of every kind of living creature. In Genesis 6:22, it is written, "Noah did everything just as God commanded him," highlighting his obedience and commitment to carrying out God's will.

While Noah is hailed for his righteousness, the Scriptures do not omit his moments of vulnerability and imperfection. In Genesis 9:20-21, after the flood subsides, Noah plants a vineyard and becomes intoxicated from the wine he produces. This incident reveals his human fallibility and serves as a reminder that even the most righteous individuals are subject to human weaknesses.

Noah's profession is described in Genesis 9:20, stating that he was a "farmer" or "tiller of the ground." As an agriculturist, he was responsible for cultivating the land and providing sustenance for his family and animals.

The construction of the Ark is a topic that has sparked debates and discussions among scholars and theologians. One question that arises is whether it is probable for Noah and his family, with no prior shipbuilding experience, to construct such an enormous vessel.

From a scientific standpoint, the construction of the Ark seems challenging for an individual or family with no maritime background. The Ark's size, around 300 cubits long (approximately 450 feet or 137 meters), would require advanced shipbuilding techniques and expertise to withstand the floodwaters and the immense stress of the catastrophic event.

Noah's character, as presented in the Scriptures, is a testament to his righteousness, faithfulness, and obedience to God. His strengths and weaknesses portray him as a relatable human figure, reminding us that even the most righteous individuals are not immune to human fallibility.

12.2 Longevity of individuals in biblical times

The likelihood of individuals living to be hundreds of years old in biblical times, as described in the genealogies of the Old Testament, is a matter of interpretation and debate. From a scientific standpoint, such extreme lifespans are highly implausible and not supported by empirical evidence or our understanding of human biology and genetics.

Modern scientific knowledge tells us that the human lifespan is limited by various biological and environmental factors, including cellular aging, genetic mutations, disease, and lifestyle. The oldest reliably documented human lifespan in modern history is around 122 years (Jeanne Calment[cix]). The idea of humans living for several centuries is not consistent with our current understanding of human biology.

Explanations for Advanced Age in Biblical Genealogies:

1. **Symbolic or Mythological Interpretation:** Some scholars and theologians propose that the advanced ages mentioned in the biblical genealogies are symbolic or mythological rather than literal. In ancient cultures, genealogies often served symbolic and theological purposes, representing ancestral lines, or establishing connections to important figures or divine beings. Long lifespans could have been used symbolically to convey the importance or significance of certain individuals or to emphasize the passage of time and the continuity of generations.

2. **Numerical Symbolism:** Numerical symbolism[cx] is common in ancient texts, including the Bible. Certain numbers, such as seven and ten, were considered sacred or symbolic and were often used to convey specific meanings. Similarly, long lifespans in the genealogies could be seen as symbolic representations of completeness, perfection, or divine favor.

3. **Different Calendar Systems:** Some researchers suggest that there might have been differences in how ages were calculated in ancient times, possibly based on different calendar systems. This could have led to a discrepancy in the reported ages compared to our modern Gregorian calendar.

4. **Transcription and Copying Errors:** The process of transmitting and copying ancient texts over centuries could have introduced errors in the recorded ages. Mistakes in copying and transcription, intentional or unintentional, might have contributed to the seemingly advanced ages in genealogies.

5. **Oral Tradition:** The early accounts in the Bible were initially transmitted through oral tradition before being written down. Oral tradition is subject to changes and elaborations over time, which might have influenced the ages mentioned in the genealogies.

While the biblical genealogies record individuals living to be hundreds of years old, the scientific plausibility of such lifespans is highly improbable. The ages mentioned in the genealogies have been the subject of diverse interpretations, including symbolic, mythological, and cultural explanations. As with many ancient texts, understanding the context, literary style, and cultural norms of the time is essential to interpret the meaning of the recorded ages in the Bible.

12.2.1   Scientific limits of human lifespan

The extraordinary lifespans attributed to individuals in biblical narratives have long fascinated scholars and readers alike. Scientific perspectives offer insights into the likelihood of such prolonged lifespans, shedding light on the possible factors contributing to biblical accounts. Several legitimate reasons support the scientific view concerning the age of individuals in biblical times.

Firstly, it is crucial to recognize the cultural and literary context of the biblical texts. Ancient societies often used symbolic numbers to convey significant meanings, and lifespans recorded in the Bible might not have been meant to be taken literally. In some cases, the ages of biblical figures may have been exaggerated for symbolic or theological purposes, rather than reflecting historical reality.

Secondly, life expectancy in ancient times was substantially lower than it is today. Infectious diseases, lack of medical knowledge, poor sanitation, limited access to clean water, and challenging living conditions were prevalent, significantly impacting human longevity. Infant mortality rates were particularly high, and children who survived infancy had a better chance of living into adulthood. However, the concept of "old age" in antiquity might have been different from modern standards.

Furthermore, genetic factors and natural selection could have played a role in shaping human longevity in biblical times. Some genetic mutations or adaptations might have conferred certain advantages, leading to individuals with specific genetic traits living longer than others. However, this would not necessarily imply individuals consistently living to several hundred years old, as portrayed in biblical narratives.

It is essential to consider the archaeological and historical evidence available for human lifespans in antiquity. While historical records and archaeological findings provide valuable insights into ancient civilizations, specific records of individuals' lifespans may not be as comprehensive or accurate as modern demographic data. Furthermore, the historical context may have influenced the documentation of ages differently across cultures and periods.

Additionally, modern scientific research in gerontology and longevity sheds light on the biological and physiological limitations of human aging. While scientific advancements have extended human life expectancy in recent centuries, there are inherent biological constraints that limit human longevity. Understanding these constraints enables us to critically evaluate the feasibility of individuals living for hundreds of years in ancient times.

The likelihood of individuals living to advanced ages in biblical times is best understood from a scientific perspective when considering cultural and literary context, ancient life expectancy, genetic factors, available historical evidence, and modern research in gerontology. It is essential to approach biblical accounts with a nuanced understanding, recognizing that symbolic numbers and theological purposes may have influenced the recorded ages. The scientific perspective offers a more comprehensive understanding of the complexity of human longevity and invites a thoughtful interpretation of the biblical narratives concerning individual lifespans.

12.2.2   *Fossil evidence for human lifespan*

The claim of humans living for hundreds of years, as depicted in biblical narratives, is a subject that has garnered both religious and scientific interest. From a scientific perspective, the fossil evidence available does not support the notion of individuals consistently living for such extended periods in ancient times. There are several reasons why this view should not be considered legitimate, based on the available fossil evidence and the understanding of human biology and lifespans.

The fossil record provides insight into the ancient populations through skeletal remains, which indicate patterns of growth, development, and mortality. Throughout human history, the average lifespan has been significantly shorter than the hundreds of years attributed to individuals in biblical times. Skeletal evidence from archaeological sites reveals that many individuals in ancient populations did not reach old age due to factors such as infectious diseases, nutritional deficiencies, and other health challenges.

Additionally, paleo demographic studies, which analyze the age distributions of skeletal populations, indicate that high infant and child mortality rates were prevalent in antiquity. This demographic pattern is inconsistent with the portrayal of consistently long lifespans among individuals in biblical narratives. The lack of a significant number of elderly individuals in ancient skeletal populations contradicts the idea of extended human lifespans.

Furthermore, advances in the study of human biology and aging have shed light on the genetic and physiological constraints of the human lifespan. While variations in lifespan can occur due to genetics, environment, and lifestyle factors, there are inherent biological limitations that affect the potential duration of human life. Genetic mutations associated with aging, cellular degeneration, and susceptibility to various age-related diseases contribute to the natural constraints on human lifespans.

Modern comparisons between human lifespans and those of our closest primate relatives, such as chimpanzees, provide additional insights. Despite sharing a common ancestor, humans generally have longer lifespans than chimpanzees. However, neither species approaches the consistently long lifespans described in biblical narratives.

The fossil evidence available from archaeological sites does not provide support for the idea of humans consistently living for hundreds of years in biblical times. Skeletal remains reveal patterns of mortality and demographic distributions that align with our understanding of the limitations on human lifespans due to biological factors and historical challenges. The absence of elderly individuals in ancient populations and the comparisons between humans and chimpanzees further undermine the legitimacy of the view that individuals in biblical times routinely lived for such extended periods.

12.2.3   Construction of the Ark with shorter lifespan

The symbolic interpretation of lifespans in biblical accounts, such as those attributed to Noah, has elicited considerable scholarly discourse at the intersection of theology and science. It becomes evident that the challenges associated with a literal interpretation of prolonged lifespans, when applied to Noah's construction of the ark, render the feasibility of such events implausible.

In the Genesis account, Noah is said to have lived for 950 years. From a biological perspective, this raises significant concerns. Contemporary knowledge of human physiology indicates that such an extended lifespan is biologically untenable. The cellular degradation, susceptibility to diseases, and metabolic limitations inherent to human biology would make it exceedingly unlikely for any individual, even in a prehistoric context, to remain functional and productive for such an extended period.

The narrative itself presents specific challenges when examining the construction of the ark. Genesis 6:14-16 provides detailed specifications for the ark's dimensions and construction materials, indicating a level of engineering sophistication that would have been influenced by the technological capabilities of the time. A prolonged lifespan for Noah would not address the logistical challenges posed by the construction itself, including sourcing materials, labor allocation, and the organization of such a monumental effort. Even with an extended lifespan, the structural integrity and resilience of the ark against environmental pressures and aging factors would remain questionable.

Reducing the timespan to construct the ark to a much shorter duration would present a different set of challenges. With a shorter lifespan, the monumental task of constructing the ark would become even more daunting. Genesis 6:3 suggests that humans would have a lifespan of 120 years. However, even within this timeframe, the intricate details of the ark's construction, the collection and organization of diverse species, and the preparation for the impending flood would strain the limits of human capability.

Considering the narrative's broader context, a shortened lifespan would require an even more accelerated pace of technological development. This raises questions about the availability of advanced tools, engineering knowledge, and construction techniques within the proposed timeline. Furthermore, the compressed timespan would exacerbate the logistical challenges, potentially leading to compromised structural integrity, inadequate preparation, and increased stress on Noah and his family.

This perspective highlights the implausibility of interpreting biblical lifespans literally in the context of Noah's construction of the ark. Whether considering extended or shortened lifespans, the challenges presented by biology, engineering, and logistics remain significant. Embracing a symbolic interpretation not only aligns more coherently with our understanding of science and human capabilities but also enriches the theological depth of the narrative, offering insights into collective endeavors, societal transitions, and the enduring human spirit.

12.3 The Nephilim

The identity and nature of the Nephilim mentioned in Genesis 6:4 have intrigued theologians, scholars, and readers for centuries, prompting various interpretations and debates. From a theological perspective, the Nephilim are commonly understood to be a group of beings resulting from the union of the "sons of God" with the "daughters of men." This interpretation has led to different views regarding the origin and nature of these beings, ranging from angelic or supernatural beings to powerful humans of exceptional stature.

The term "Nephilim" is derived from the Hebrew word "Nephilim"[cxi], which can be translated as "fallen ones" or "giants." This term appears only a few times in the Bible, including the passage in Genesis 6:4. The context of this verse suggests that the Nephilim were on the earth both before and after the "sons of God" took human wives, indicating their existence as a distinct group that continued even after the flood. The subsequent narrative does not provide extensive details about the Nephilim, leaving room for theological speculation and interpretation.

From a theological perspective, the Nephilim align with Adam and Eve in the sense that they all form part of the broader narrative of human history and the complexities of the fallen world. Adam and Eve, as the first human beings created by God, are pivotal figures in the biblical narrative, representing the origin of humanity and the introduction of sin into the world. The Nephilim, if understood as offspring of the "sons of God" and the "daughters of men," is connected to the theme of disobedience and corruption in the pre-flood world.

In this context, the Nephilim's alignment with Adam and Eve underscores the theme of human rebellion and the consequences of moral choices. Just as Adam and Eve's disobedience led to the fall of humanity, the potential transgressions of the Nephilim and their unique origins are indicative of the broader fallen state of creation. This alignment highlights the consistent biblical narrative of sin, judgment, and the need for redemption throughout human history.

While the specific nature and identity of the Nephilim remain subject to theological interpretation, their presence in the Genesis narrative serves as a reminder of the complexities of the biblical worldview and the broader themes of human choices, divine intervention, and the unfolding plan of redemption. Theologians often engage in textual analysis, linguistic studies, and comparative readings of related passages to develop a comprehensive understanding of Nephilim's theological implications within the biblical context.

12.4 Vegetation watered "from below"

The passage in Genesis 2:5-6, which speaks of a time when "no plant of the field had yet sprung up because the Lord God had not sent rain on the earth and there was no one to work the ground, but streams came up from the earth and watered the whole surface of the ground," presents an intriguing intersection of scientific and theological considerations. This verse has been examined through both natural processes and theological symbolism, shedding light on its broader implications.

From a scientific perspective, the description in Genesis 2:5-6 could align with the idea of subterranean water sources, such as springs or aquifers, providing the necessary moisture for the earth's surface before the widespread availability of rain. In some geographical areas, underground water sources can indeed emerge from the ground, supplying moisture to plants without relying solely on rainwater. This aligns with the concept of localized irrigation systems through natural springs, which would have facilitated the growth of vegetation in a pre-rain environment.

From a theological perspective, this passage highlights God's provision and creative design in sustaining the earth's ecosystems. The imagery of water emerging from the ground underscores God's nurturing care for creation even in the absence of rain. This theological symbolism reflects themes of divine providence and the interplay between the physical world and God's sustaining presence. Just as God provided water from the earth to nourish the ground, this passage can be understood as a precursor to the broader biblical narrative of God's ongoing provision for humanity and creation.

Examples from the Bible further support the theological significance of water as a symbol of God's life-giving presence. In Psalm 104:10-13, the psalmist celebrates God's role as the source of water for the earth: "He sends the springs into the valleys; they flow among the hills. They give drink to every beast of the field; the wild donkeys quench their thirst. By them the birds of the heavens have their home; they sing among the branches." This imagery reinforces the concept of God's provision through water, both from the ground and through other means.

Genesis 2:5-6 offers a unique perspective on the early stage of the earth's ecosystem, emphasizing the significance of water in sustaining creation. From a scientific standpoint, the emergence of water from subterranean sources provides a plausible explanation for the described phenomenon. From a theological standpoint, this passage underscores God's creative provision and care for the earth, aligning with broader biblical themes of divine sustenance. The symbolism of water in this context is echoed throughout the Bible, reinforcing the theological depth of the passage.

12.5 Did life exist after the flood?

The narrative of the Great Flood in Genesis 8:8-12, specifically the episode where a dove brings back an olive leaf to Noah, prompts intriguing scientific inquiries regarding the likelihood of trees and vegetation surviving after a year of submersion in saltwater. While the story carries theological significance, exploring this aspect from a scientific perspective offers insights into the challenges posed by the ecological conditions presented in the account.

From a scientific standpoint, the survival of trees and vegetation in saltwater conditions for an extended period presents significant challenges. Saltwater, which has a higher salinity than most land-based plants can tolerate, can lead to osmotic stress. This stress occurs as saltwater draws water away from plant cells, causing dehydration and eventual cell death. Moreover, saltwater exposure can hinder the uptake of essential nutrients, further compromising plant health.

In the context of the Great Flood, the account suggests that the entire Earth was covered in water for a year (Genesis 7:24, Genesis 8:14). This would entail not only saltwater inundation but also the prolonged absence of sunlight necessary for photosynthesis, a vital process for plant survival. Lack of sunlight would lead to an inability to produce energy, weakening the plants and reducing their chances of recovery.

The retrieval of an olive leaf by the dove in Genesis 8:8-12 is symbolic and theologically significant, indicating the receding of the floodwaters and the eventual renewal of the Earth. However, from a scientific perspective, the survival of trees and vegetation in such conditions is highly implausible. The challenges of osmotic stress, nutrient deficiency, and the absence of sunlight make it improbable for vegetation to survive for a year submerged in saltwater.

It's important to note that the theological value of the narrative doesn't necessarily depend on the ecological feasibility of vegetation survival. The Genesis account serves to convey theological truths, including God's covenant with creation and the promise of renewal. The olive leaf serves as a symbol of hope and divine providence, even if its biological plausibility is limited by scientific constraints.

Examining the likelihood of trees and vegetation surviving in saltwater conditions during the Flood from a scientific perspective reveals ecological challenges that cast doubt on their survival. While the theological message of the story remains intact, the ecological realities emphasize the symbolic nature of the narrative and the interplay between theology and science. This exploration underscores the nuanced nature of religious texts, prompting both believers and scholars to engage with their theological and scientific dimensions.

12.6 Who can presume to know the mind of God?

The statement in Genesis 8:21-22, where Yahweh declares to Himself that He will not bring a flood on the earth again while enjoying the fragrance of the burnt offerings, raises intriguing theological questions about the nature of divine communication and human understanding of the mind of God. This passage presents a significant instance of divine revelation, provoking reflections on how humans perceive and interpret the intentions of the divine.

In Genesis 8:21-22, Yahweh's decision is linked to the pleasing aroma of Noah's burnt offerings, signifying Noah's obedience and devotion. Yahweh's declaration serves as a divine response to the offerings and reflects a profound theological message about divine mercy and covenant. The passage underscores the establishment of a covenant between God and humanity, emphasizing God's commitment to maintaining the order of creation and refraining from another global flood. This divine promise encompasses not only humanity but also all living creatures, showcasing God's concern for the entirety of creation.

However, the narrative's exploration of Yahweh's thoughts and intentions in this passage invites theological contemplation about human limitations in comprehending the divine mind. The question arises: How do humans come to know God's inner thoughts? The answer lies in the concept of divine revelation. Throughout Scripture, God communicates with humans through various means, including direct dialogues, dreams, visions, and inspired writings. Divine revelation allows humans to gain insights into God's nature, will, and purposes that would otherwise remain beyond human comprehension.

It's crucial to recognize that divine revelation is not equivalent to human presumption or a mere projection of human thoughts onto the divine. Instead, it's a gift bestowed by God, enabling humans to glimpse aspects of God's intentions. This revelation occurs within the framework of God's self-disclosure and interaction with creation. The Bible itself is considered a primary source of divine revelation, providing insights into God's character, attributes, and intentions.

In the context of Genesis 8:21-22, the passage serves to emphasize the enduring covenant between God and creation. The statement reflects God's inner disposition and divine will, communicated to humanity through inspired writing. While humans cannot fully grasp the mind of God, divine revelation offers a way for them to gain understanding and insight into

God's purposes and intentions. The narrative of the burnt offerings and God's promise highlights the interconnectedness between divine communication, human response, and the unfolding of God's redemptive plan

The statement in Genesis 8:21-22 presents a theological exploration of divine revelation and human understanding of the mind of God. The passage illustrates how divine intentions and promises are conveyed to humanity through inspired writings and other means of communication. While humans cannot fully fathom the depths of the divine mind, divine revelation provides a glimpse into God's nature and purposes, fostering a relationship of trust and dialogue between the Creator and creation. This interplay between the divine and the human underscores the richness of theological reflection on biblical narratives.

12.7 The immutable nature of God

The immutability of God, a fundamental tenet in theology, asserts that God is unchanging in nature, essence, and character. This concept finds its roots in various religious traditions and has been a subject of profound theological contemplation.

One of the primary reasons to consider the immutability of God as legitimate is its philosophical consistency. If God were to change, it would imply that there is an external force or cause influencing Him. Such a proposition raises questions about God's omnipotence and sovereignty. The immutable nature of God safeguards the idea of a self-sufficient and independent divine being, whose actions and attributes remain constant across time and circumstances.

God's immutability is closely connected to the idea of divine perfection. If God were subject to change, it could imply either improvement or decline in His nature. Both scenarios challenge the concept of an eternally perfect and all-knowing being. Embracing the immutable nature of God reinforces the belief in an eternally perfect and unblemished entity, free from any imperfections.

Many religious texts, such as the Bible, the Quran, and the Vedas, explicitly affirm the unchanging nature of God. For instance, the Bible states in Malachi 3:6, "For I the Lord do not change." This assertion aligns with the belief that God's essence remains constant throughout eternity. Such scriptural affirmations provide a robust theological basis for the immutable nature of God.

The immutability of God is essential to reconcile the concepts of God's omnipresence and eternality. If God were subject to change, there would be moments when He would not be fully present or cease to exist, which contradicts the notions of God's eternal and omnipresent nature. The immutability of God ensures a consistent and continuous divine presence that transcends temporal boundaries.

The belief in God's immutability finds support in the idea of divine faithfulness and reliability. If God were to change, His promises and commitments could become uncertain or unreliable. However, acknowledging God's unchanging nature affirms His steadfastness in keeping His word, providing comfort and assurance to believers in times of adversity.

The concept of God's immutability also applies to His moral standards and principles. If God's nature were to change, moral truths might become relative and unstable. However, the belief in the unchanging nature of God provides a firm foundation for objective moral values and a consistent moral framework.

From a theological perspective, the concept of the immutable nature of God stands as a legitimate and essential principle in various religious traditions. Philosophical consistency, divine perfection, scriptural foundations, and alignment with divine attributes like omnipresence and eternality all bolster the case for this view. Moreover, the concept affirms the faithfulness of God and provides a stable foundation for moral truths. As theologians continue to delve deeper into the mysteries of God, the notion of God's immutability remains a profound and enduring aspect of divine theology.

12.7.1   The Nature of God in Genesis

The concept of an immutable God seems to conflict with God expressing regret or changing His mind in certain biblical passages, such as in Genesis 6:6-9, which poses complex theological questions about God's nature and actions. It is important to approach these verses with an understanding of the literary and theological context of the narrative.

The anthropomorphic language used in the Scriptures is one way of explaining divine actions in human terms to make them more understandable to us. God's expressions of regret or sorrow should not be understood in the same way human emotions are experienced. God's regret is likely intended to convey a response to human behavior and choices, rather than a change in His divine nature.

Moreover, the concept of God regretting His actions raises the theological question of divine sovereignty versus human free will. The Scriptures often present a tension between God's sovereignty and human responsibility, and the account of the flood may be seen as an example of this tension. God, in His foreknowledge, may have known that humanity would become increasingly sinful, leading to the regretful decision to send the flood. However, this does not negate human responsibility for their actions.

Regarding the statement that God saw His creation as "good" in the early chapters of Genesis, it is essential to recognize that the goodness of creation does not imply a guarantee of perfection or immutability. The goodness of creation refers to its inherent purpose and order as established by God. The entrance of sin and corruption through human choices disrupted the goodness of creation but did not negate its original purpose.

The account of the flood does not imply that animals or young children were inherently sinful. Rather, it appears to be a judgment on the rampant evil and wickedness that permeated human society at that time. God's decision to destroy all living things may be understood as a response to humanity's actions, as the flood was a consequence of human sinfulness.

Regarding death, the concept of the Fall and its consequences is a matter of theological interpretation. Some traditions understand death as a direct result of human sin and disobedience, while others interpret it differently. The flood narrative does not necessarily negate or confirm the theological interpretations of the Fall; it serves as a distinct event in the biblical narrative with its theological implications.

The depiction of God expressing regret or changing His mind in certain passages invites deep theological contemplation and raises questions about the nature of God's omniscience, sovereignty, and human responsibility. These narratives should be understood in the broader theological context of the Scriptures and the complexities of human-divine relationships.

The account of the flood, like many biblical passages, prompts readers to grapple with profound theological and philosophical issues while recognizing the depth and mystery of God's divine nature.

12.7.2   The Tower of Babel

The story of the Tower of Babel, found in Genesis 11, presents a complex portrayal of God's character that seems to contrast with the message conveyed in John 3:16. In the Tower of Babel narrative, humanity unites to build a tower that reaches the heavens, challenging God's authority (Genesis 11:4). In response, God confuses their language, scattering them across the earth and halting their ambitious project (Genesis 11:7-9). This account has led some to question whether the God depicted here is capricious, as He was when He regretted creating humankind in the story of the Flood (Genesis 6:6-7).

John 3:16, on the other hand, is a well-known verse from the New Testament that reveals a different facet of God's character. It states, "For God so loved the world that he gave his one and only Son, that whoever believes in him shall not perish but have eternal life." Here, God's love, sacrifice, and redemption stand at the forefront, painting a picture of a compassionate and merciful deity who seeks to reconcile humanity to Himself.

The juxtaposition of these two narratives raises important theological considerations. The perceived capriciousness of God in the Tower of Babel narrative stems from the divine response to human arrogance and defiance. However, this portrayal should be interpreted within the broader context of God's sovereignty and desire for humanity's well-being. While the confusion of languages may appear harsh, it can also be seen as a corrective measure aimed at preventing unchecked human pride and promoting diversity, which is crucial for the flourishing of human society.

When contrasted with John 3:16, the perception of capriciousness in these narratives is challenged. John 3:16 encapsulates the essence of God's love for humanity, offering salvation through Christ's sacrificial death. This passage paints a theological portrait of a God who desires reconciliation, not condemnation.

Ultimately, the juxtaposition of the Tower of Babel and John 3:16 calls for a nuanced understanding of God's character within the biblical narrative. God's actions and emotions are conveyed in response to the context of human actions and choices. Theological reflection on these narratives encourages a holistic view of God—one that encompasses justice, compassion, sovereignty, and a redemptive plan for humanity's salvation. Through a comprehensive examination of these passages, believers can deepen their understanding of God's multifaceted character and engage in a more robust theological discourse.

Theological perspectives that frame God as capricious based on the Tower of Babel narrative may overlook the broader context of divine interaction with humanity throughout the Bible. The Old Testament depicts a progressive revelation of God's character, culminating in the New Testament revelation of God's redemptive love in Christ. The perceived tension between God's actions in the Old and New Testaments can be understood as part of humanity's evolving relationship with the divine—a relationship marked by both discipline and grace.

The apparent contradiction between God's actions in the Tower of Babel and John 3:16 necessitates a holistic theological approach. It calls for an examination of God's actions within the context of His overarching plan for creation and humanity's journey toward salvation. When viewed through this lens, the portrayal of God's character becomes a tapestry of justice, mercy, compassion, and divine purpose. Rather than seeing God as capricious, these narratives invite believers to engage in a deeper exploration of the dynamic interplay between divine sovereignty and human agency, as well as the profound depths of God's love and grace.

It should also be stated that the actions of a capricious god in the story of the Tower of Babel are contrary to the story in Acts 2:5-13 where at Pentecost the Holy Spirit brought unity and allowed people of various tongues to understand the Gospel message preached by the apostles in their language.

12.7.3   An evolving understanding of God

The biblical narrative unfolds as a dynamic journey of humanity's evolving understanding of God's nature, revealing His profound love and redemptive plan for creation. This divine revelation progressively deepens, as exemplified in passages such as John 3:16 and Acts 2:5-13, offering insights into the transformative relationship between God and His people.

John 3:16 encapsulates a pivotal moment in the Gospel of John, emphasizing God's unconditional love and salvific intention. "For God so loved the world that he gave his one and only Son, that whoever believes in him shall not perish but have eternal life." This verse underscores God's divine plan for salvation through Jesus Christ, showcasing a more intimate portrayal of God as a loving Father who extends mercy and redemption to all of humanity.

Acts 2:5-13 recounts the event of Pentecost, when the Holy Spirit descended upon the apostles, enabling them to speak in various languages. The multitude of people who gathered were amazed and perplexed, recognizing the divine intervention at play. This event reflects an evolving understanding of God's nature as a universal presence that transcends linguistic and cultural boundaries. The Holy Spirit's manifestation signifies a transformative moment in the apostles' understanding, as they begin to realize the breadth of God's reach and His desire to engage with people from all walks of life.

Throughout the biblical narrative, humanity's perception of God evolves from a more distant, awe-inspiring deity to a personal and compassionate Father. In the Old Testament, God's interactions with humanity are often characterized by awe and reverence. For instance, in the story of Moses and the burning bush (Exodus 3:1-6), God's presence is so overwhelming that Moses hides his face. This encounter portrays God as holy and unapproachable, reinforcing the concept of divine transcendence.

However, as the narrative progresses, the revelations become more intimate and relational. The Incarnation of Jesus Christ is the pinnacle of this transformation, exemplifying God's desire to bridge the gap between divinity and humanity. Through the life, death, and resurrection of Jesus, humanity gains a profound understanding of God's sacrificial love and His willingness to share in human suffering.

This perspective recognizes the evolving understanding of God's nature throughout the biblical narrative. John 3:16 and Acts 2:5-13 serve as crucial milestones, depicting the shift from a distant and awe-inspiring God to a loving and merciful Father who actively seeks a personal relationship with His creation. This transformation culminates in the revelation of God's ultimate expression of love through Jesus Christ, affirming the enduring theme of divine love and redemption that permeates the entirety of Scripture.

12.8 The importance of Genesis

The value of believing in the entirety of the Bible, even in the presence of scientific inconsistencies, is rooted in a holistic understanding of Scripture's purpose and its multifaceted nature. While some passages, especially in the book of Genesis, may not align seamlessly with scientific knowledge, they are intended to convey profound spiritual truths, moral teachings, and theological insights that transcend the boundaries of empirical observation.

The book of Genesis, serving as the foundational narrative of creation, holds a special place in this discussion. Genesis offers an allegorical account of the origins of the cosmos and humanity, emphasizing God's role as the Creator and the inherent dignity of human beings as made in His image (Genesis 1:26-27). While modern scientific discoveries present alternative explanations of the origins of the universe and human life, the symbolic significance of Genesis remains undiminished. The focus shifts from a literal interpretation of the six-day creation to a deeper exploration of divine intentionality and the foundational truth that God is the source of all existence.

In the Catholic tradition, the Church Fathers and theologians have often interpreted Genesis in an allegorical or symbolic manner, recognizing that its primary purpose is to convey spiritual and theological truths rather than to provide a scientific treatise. St. Augustine[cxii], for instance, in his work "The Literal Meaning of Genesis"[cxiii], argued that the creation narrative should be understood in a way that harmonizes with reason and scientific understanding while preserving its spiritual significance.

Believing in the entirety of the Bible, including passages that might seem inconsistent with scientific knowledge, fosters a profound reverence for the divine inspiration of Scripture. The Second Vatican Council's document "Dei Verbum" emphasizes the dual authorship of the Bible: both divine and human. As such, Scripture employs various literary forms, including myth, poetry, history, and prophecy, to convey its messages. Genesis, utilizing symbolic language, underscores humanity's need for God, the reality of sin, and the promise of redemption, themes that echo throughout salvation history.

Rather than viewing scientific inconsistencies as challenges to faith, the Catholic perspective encourages believers to engage in a nuanced and thoughtful approach that recognizes the different modes of expression employed in Scripture. While empirical science and faith are distinct realms of inquiry, they need not be incompatible. The value lies in embracing both dimensions—scientific exploration and spiritual reflection—as complementary ways of encountering the profound mysteries of existence and the Divine.

The value of believing in the entirety of the Bible, including Genesis and its potential scientific inconsistencies, resides in recognizing the multifaceted nature of Scripture and its capacity to convey deeper spiritual truths. Genesis, as an allegorical narrative, invites believers to ponder the divine purpose behind creation, humanity's relationship with God, and the unfolding plan of redemption. Embracing this perspective fosters a richer engagement with Scripture and a deeper appreciation for the harmonious interplay between faith and reason.

13 <u>Climate Change</u>

13.1 Creationist and Fundamentalist Views

From a Creationist perspective, the discourse surrounding global warming is often viewed within a broader framework of stewardship and dominion over creation, as outlined in the book of Genesis. Creationists acknowledge the reality of climate change but interpret its causes and implications through their understanding of Scripture. The biblical mandate to exercise responsible dominion over the Earth (Genesis 1:26-28) is seen as a call to care for and manage the planet's resources, including its environment.

Creationists often highlight God's promise to Noah after the Flood, found in Genesis 8:22: "While the earth remains, seedtime and harvest, cold and heat, summer and winter, day and night, shall not cease." This passage is interpreted as a divine assurance of the Earth's stability and order, suggesting that while climate variations may occur, the planet's overall conditions will remain within certain bounds. Creationists maintain that while human activities can influence the environment, God's providence and design ensure that the Earth will not experience catastrophic changes beyond His ordained plan.

When it comes to supporting their view on global warming, Creationists often point to natural climate variability, highlighting that Earth's climate has experienced fluctuations throughout history. They emphasize that while human activity can contribute to localized environmental changes, the global impact might be less significant than mainstream climate models suggest. Creationists also draw attention to uncertainties in climate science and question the extent to which human actions are solely responsible for current climate trends.

The Fundamentalist perspective on global warming is rooted in a belief in the divine sovereignty and ultimate control of the Creator over the Earth's processes. Fundamentalists regard the environment as part of God's creation, and they view the Earth's climate as a system governed by God's design. While acknowledging the potential for human impact on the environment, Fundamentalists often emphasize the limitations of human understanding in predicting complex climate patterns.

Fundamentalists draw upon Scriptural references to God's providence and control over nature. Passages like Psalm 104 highlight the Creator's role in sustaining the Earth's ecosystems and cycles: "You cause the grass to grow for the livestock and plants for man to cultivate, that he may bring forth food from the earth" (Psalm 104:14). This perspective underscores the belief that the Earth's climate is intricately woven into God's creative design and that natural variations, including climate fluctuations, are under His ultimate governance.

From the Fundamentalist viewpoint, concerns about global warming might be perceived as an expression of God's call for stewardship and responsible care of the Earth. While acknowledging that human activities can impact the environment, Fundamentalists emphasize that God's providence remains constant even in the face of uncertainties and challenges posed by changing climates.

Both the Creationist and Fundamentalist perspectives on global warming are shaped by their theological beliefs about God's sovereignty, creation, and human responsibility. While these perspectives may lead to skepticism or caution regarding certain aspects of mainstream climate science, they also underscore the importance of responsible stewardship and trust in God's providence amidst the complexities of our changing world.

13.2 Evidence of human-caused climate change

Global warming, as a phenomenon driven by the accumulation of greenhouse gases in the Earth's atmosphere, is firmly established within the realm of scientific consensus. Extensive research and empirical evidence substantiate the reality of rising global temperatures and their far-reaching consequences. This scientific perspective rests on a foundation of interdisciplinary studies encompassing climatology, atmospheric science, and data analysis.

Temperature records constitute a compelling piece of evidence for global warming. Over the past century, global average temperatures have exhibited a consistent upward trend. This warming trend is evident in temperature records from both land-based and satellite measurements. For instance, the National Aeronautics and Space Administration (NASA) and the National Oceanic and Atmospheric Administration (NOAA)[cxiv] compile and analyze temperature data, consistently showing increasing temperatures since the late 19th century.

Further evidence arises from the retreat of glaciers and the reduction of ice cover in polar regions. Glacier melting rates have accelerated in recent decades, leading to reduced ice volumes and sea-level rise. Satellite observations of polar ice caps also reveal a decline in Arctic Sea ice extent, contributing to concerns about rising sea levels. These trends are closely aligned with global warming predictions stemming from climate models that incorporate greenhouse gas emissions.

Perhaps the most telling evidence comes from the analysis of greenhouse gas concentrations. Carbon dioxide (CO_2), methane (CH4), and other greenhouse gases trap heat in the Earth's atmosphere, contributing to the greenhouse effect. The Mauna Loa Observatory[cxv] in Hawaii has documented the consistent increase in atmospheric CO2 concentrations since the Industrial Revolution, correlating with the burning of fossil fuels. Similarly, ice core samples[cxvi] from Antarctica and Greenland provide historical records of atmospheric CO2 levels, indicating a substantial increase since pre-industrial times.

Extreme weather events also bear witness to the impact of global warming. Intense hurricanes, heatwaves, droughts, and heavy rainfall events have been linked to changing climatic patterns influenced by the Earth's warming. These events reflect the complex interactions within the climate system, demonstrating the multifaceted consequences of global warming.

Scientific organizations worldwide, such as the Intergovernmental Panel on Climate Change (IPCC)[cxvii], have consistently affirmed the validity of global warming through comprehensive assessments of scientific literature. Peer-reviewed studies, modeling, and data analysis converge to form a robust scientific consensus on the reality of anthropogenic global warming.

Regarding climate change, the scientific consensus, supported by extensive research and data, points to human activities, particularly the burning of fossil fuels and deforestation, as significant drivers of the current climate crisis. The overwhelming majority of climate scientists agree that the Earth is experiencing rapid and unprecedented warming primarily due to human-induced greenhouse gas emissions. This anthropogenic climate change is resulting in rising sea levels, extreme weather events, and disruptions to ecosystems, with serious implications for the planet's biodiversity and human societies.

The validity of global warming from a purely scientific perspective is supported by a wealth of empirical evidence across various domains. Temperature records, ice melt rates, greenhouse gas concentrations, and extreme weather events all contribute to the consensus understanding of a warming planet. The interdisciplinary nature of climate science, coupled with the rigorous examination of data and empirical research, underscores the urgency of addressing this pressing global issue.

13.3 A quote from my Mom

When faced with a challenging situation, my Mom was fond of saying, "Pray as everything depends on God, and act like everything depends on you!". That's great advice, Mom! Let's hope that we can act on climate change before it is too late. Although, I am afraid we have already passed the tipping point.

Rather than aggressively working as stewards of the planet for the benefit of future generations, too many individuals deny the reality of what we see so clearly around us choosing instead to deny climate change and view it as a hoax.

14 <u>Conclusion</u>

14.1 Recapitulation of key points

Christianity provides a panorama of intricate theological and scientific insights, encompassing the viewpoints of Creationist, Fundamentalist, Catholic, and scientific lenses. Scripture provides the essence of these perspectives, emphasizing their interplay in advancing our comprehension of creation, human origins, ethics, and divine-human interaction.

Creationist, Fundamentalist, Catholic, and scientific viewpoints intersect, creating a dynamic tapestry and discourse that enriches our understanding of the cosmos, human existence, and divine interaction. This interdisciplinary exploration highlights the complexity of faith and reason, inviting ongoing dialogue that shapes the evolution of theological and scientific thought.

14.2 Need for continued exploration and discussion

The exploration of the intersections between Creationist, Fundamentalist, Catholic, and scientific perspectives within the context of Genesis narratives underscores the necessity for continued examination and dialogue. These diverse viewpoints contribute to a broader understanding of creation, human origins, ethics, and the divine-human relationship. Such ongoing discussions foster intellectual growth, spiritual enrichment, and the evolution of thought within both religious and scientific communities.

The exploration of Creationist, Fundamentalist, Catholic, and scientific perspectives within the Genesis narratives necessitates a continuous need for exploration and discussion.

The convergence of these viewpoints enriches our understanding of the cosmos, human existence, and the divine. As these discussions persist, they not only enhance our comprehension of the intersection between faith and reason but also shape the ongoing evolution of religious and scientific thought.

14.3 Embracing theological and scientific diversity

The imperative to embrace the richness of theological and scientific diversity within the exploration of Genesis narratives resonates as a crucial aspect of advancing holistic understanding. Engaging with Creationists, Fundamentalist, Catholic, and scientific perspectives opens doors to a broader comprehension of creation, human origins, ethics, and divine-human interaction. Such inclusivity fosters intellectual growth, encourages interfaith dialogue, and deepens the integration of faith and reason.

The need to embrace the richness of theological and scientific diversity emerges as a fundamental principle within the exploration of Genesis narratives. Engaging with Fundamentalist, Catholic, and scientific perspectives promotes unity, mutual learning, and interdisciplinary dialogue.

This inclusivity contributes to a comprehensive understanding of the cosmos, human existence, and the divine, reflecting the intricate tapestry of faith and reason. As these diverse viewpoints converge, they illuminate the dynamic interplay between the sacred and the scientific, enriching our understanding of Genesis narratives and the profound questions they address.

14.4 A call for consistency and logic

In the spirit of unity and understanding, it is essential to recognize the sincere beliefs of Creationists, Fundamentalists, and individuals who adhere to scientific perspectives. There has been considerable effort to reconcile these various viewpoints, often with the intent of harmonizing them with unique interpretations of the world. However, it is evident that the scientific interpretation of the universe and the literal readings of certain biblical passages can sometimes pose challenges in fitting together seamlessly.

It is worth acknowledging that salvation is not predicated upon a strict adherence to the principle of Sola Scriptura, which asserts the Bible's sole authority in matters of faith and practice. The foundation of our salvation lies in the redemptive sacrifice of Jesus Christ, while the Bible remains a guide that provides infallible insights into matters of faith and morality.

While Romans 10:13-14 and John 3:3 are frequently emphasized by Creationists and Fundamentalists in discussions of literal interpretation, the Bread of Life discourse in John 6:26-71 presents another layer of significance. Here, Jesus articulates six times the necessity of consuming His flesh and blood to attain eternal life, unambiguously stating that this mandate is not symbolic but literal.

The concept of Transubstantiation[cxviii], as understood by the Catholic Church, underscores the literal interpretation of Jesus' words in the Bread of Life discourse. This view aligns with the Church's historical continuity and Apostolic authority, as demonstrated in the codification of the Bible during the Synod of Hippo[cxix] in 393 AD.

Acknowledging diversity, the Second Vatican Council's[cxx] document "Lumen Gentium"[cxxi] recognizes elements of truth and holiness in other religions, suggesting that individuals who are not formally part of the Catholic Church can be oriented towards salvation. This inclusivity is a reminder that God's mercy transcends all denominational boundaries.

Catholics believe that Jesus paid a debt He didn't owe, because we owed a debt we couldn't pay. Catholics acknowledge that there is nothing an individual can do to merit salvation, neither profession of faith, words, or actions. Instead, there is complete and total reliance on God's mercy for our undeserved salvation.

On my day of judgement, when I stand before my Creator, I will plead for mercy, not justice.

15 <u>References</u>

For those who may have a printed copy I am aware that hyperlinks do not work in printed media and for that purpose, in this section I am including the resource links I used in compiling this book. I chose to add the links as endnotes instead of footnotes because I thought the lengthy footnotes were not aesthetically pleasing amid the text and led to disruption of thought while reading.

I understand that typing links as they appear below can be vexing. I would suggest that in such instances you simply do an Internet search of the topic, since most often there is nothing unique about the precise reference I have cited.

If that method is not satisfactory, please feel free to email me profjim@email.com and I will respond back with a PDF copy of this book which contains the links. From the bottom of my heart, thank you so very much for taking the time to read this book.

---

[i] https://www.youtube.com/watch?v=z6kgvhG3Akl

[ii] https://www.icr.org/henry_morris/

[iii] https://en.wikipedia.org/wiki/Ken_Ham

[iv] https://www.amazon.com/s?k=the+genesis+flood&hvadid=616990801337&hvdev=c&hvlocphy=9016884&hvnetw=g&hvqmt=e&hvrand=12870030268015519958&hvtargid=kwd-494334935&hydadcr=24658_13611734&tag=googhydr-20&ref=pd_sl_69iq73qxbw_e

[v] https://www.amazon.com/s?k=the+answers+book&hvadid=616863042231&hvdev=c&hvlocphy=9016884&hvnetw=g&hvqmt=e&hvrand=84605141011718

20073&hvtargid=kwd-810190505&hydadcr=24659_13611768&tag=googhydr-20&ref=pd_sl_3l7eyuzief_e

vi https://www.vatican.va/archive/ENG0015/_INDEX.HTM

vii https://scepterpublishers.org/collections/navarre-bibles

viii Seven C's of History | Answers in Genesis

ix History - Wikipedia

x https://georgesjournal.net/2019/08/15/what-is-historical-science/

xi Deceitful Terms—Historical and Observational Science | Answers in Genesis

xii https://www.amazon.com/Interlinear-Bible-Hebrew-Greek-English-English-Hebrew/dp/1565639774

xiii https://www.amazon.com/Strongs-Exhaustive-Concordance-James-Strong/dp/0785250565/ref=pd_lpo_sccl_2/136-6852724-2227902?pd_rd_w=ndcSD&content-id=amzn1.sym.116f529c-aa4d-4763-b2b6-4d614ec7dc00&pf_rd_p=116f529c-aa4d-4763-b2b6-4d614ec7dc00&pf_rd_r=BXMY79XAB0XVCGB236CW&pd_rd_wg=ptRnN&pd_rd_r=c3609401-0b2a-425e-9591-106a55c96fea&pd_rd_i=0785250565&psc=1

xiv https://www.amazon.com/Vines-Expository-Dictionary-Testament-Words/dp/0785250549

xv https://www.amazon.com/Matthew-Henrys-Commentary-Whole-Bible/dp/1598564366

xvi https://www.logos.com/product/55024/the-new-american-commentary-series

xvii Exegesis - Wikipedia

xviii Eisegesis - Wikipedia

xix Hermeneutics - Wikipedia

xx Semiotics - Wikipedia

xxi Literary criticism - Wikipedia

xxii
https://en.wikipedia.org/wiki/Sola_scriptura#:~:text=Sola%20scriptura%20(La
tin%20for%20'by,for%20Christian%20faith%20and%20practice.

xxiii
https://www.vatican.va/archive/hist_councils/ii_vatican_council/documents/va
t-ii_const_19651118_dei-verbum_en.html

xxiv https://en.wikipedia.org/wiki/Documentary_hypothesis

xxv https://biblearchaeologyreport.com/2019/02/22/three-ancient-near-
eastern-creation-myths/

xxvi https://en.wikipedia.org/wiki/Talmud

xxvii https://en.wikipedia.org/wiki/Mishnah

xxviii https://en.wikipedia.org/wiki/Augustine_of_Hippo

xxix https://en.wikipedia.org/wiki/Origen

xxx https://en.wikipedia.org/wiki/Jerome

xxxi
https://en.wikipedia.org/wiki/Ancient_Near_Eastern_Texts_Relating_to_the_
Old_Testament

xxxii https://en.wikipedia.org/wiki/James_Ussher

xxxiii https://en.wikipedia.org/wiki/Big_Bang

xxxiv https://naturalhistory.si.edu/education/teaching-resources/life-
science/early-life-earth-animal-
origins#:~:text=The%20earliest%20life%20forms%20we,about%203.7%20bil
lion%20years%20old.

xxxv https://en.wikipedia.org/wiki/Cambrian_explosion

xxxvi https://www.nps.gov/subjects/geology/time-scale.htm

xxxvii https://www.nature.com/scitable/knowledge/library/comparative-genomics-13239404/

xxxviii DNA - Wikipedia

xxxix https://solarsystem.nasa.gov/solar-system/our-solar-system/in-depth/#:~:text=Our%20solar%20system%20formed%20about,spinning%2C%20swirling%20disk%20of%20material.

xl
https://nature.berkeley.edu/garbelottoat/?p=582#:~:text=The%20Miller%2DUrey%20experiment%20was,the%20theoretical%20ideas%20of%20A.I.

xli https://en.wikipedia.org/wiki/RNA_world

xlii Ribonucleic Acid (RNA) (genome.gov)

xliii
https://www.lpi.usra.edu/science/kring/epo_web/impact_cratering/origin_of_life/index.html

xliv Radiometric dating - Wikipedia

xlv https://en.wikipedia.org/wiki/Geochronology

xlvi https://www.thoughtco.com/uranium-lead-dating-1440810

xlvii https://www.sciencedirect.com/topics/earth-and-planetary-sciences/potassium-argon-dating

xlviii https://en.wikipedia.org/wiki/Olduvai_Gorge

xlix https://en.wikipedia.org/wiki/Rubidium%E2%80%93strontium_dating

l https://en.wikipedia.org/wiki/Sudbury_Basin

li https://en.wikipedia.org/wiki/Sudbury_Basin

lii https://www.sciencedirect.com/topics/earth-and-planetary-sciences/multicollector-inductively-coupled-plasma-mass-spectrometry

liii https://en.wikipedia.org/wiki/Samarium%E2%80%93neodymium_dating

liv https://en.wikipedia.org/wiki/Argon%E2%80%93argon_dating

lv https://www.ncbi.nlm.nih.gov/books/NBK208869/

lvi https://en.wikipedia.org/wiki/Luminescence_dating

lvii https://www.fossilera.com/pages/dating-fossils

lviii https://en.wikipedia.org/wiki/Geomagnetic_reversal

lix http://www-odp.tamu.edu/publications/198_IR/chap_02/c2_6.htm

lx https://www.scientificamerican.com/article/the-age-of-the-ocean/

lxi https://illinois.pbslearningmedia.org/resource/ess05.sci.ess.eiu.moon/the-origin-of-the-moon/

lxii https://en.wikipedia.org/wiki/Late_Heavy_Bombardment

lxiii https://www.space.com/earth-moon-different-compositions-surprise.html

lxiv https://en.wikipedia.org/wiki/Hubble_Space_Telescope

lxv https://www.nationalgeographic.com/science/article/spitzer-space-telescope

lxvi
https://en.wikipedia.org/wiki/Gravitational_collapse#:~:text=Gravitational%20collapse%20is%20the%20contraction,structure%20formation%20in%20the%20universe.

lxvii https://en.wikipedia.org/wiki/Herbig%E2%80%93Haro_object

lxviii
https://en.wikipedia.org/wiki/Stellar_evolution#:~:text=A%20stellar%20evolutionary%20model%20is,temperature%20are%20the%20only%20constraints.

lxix https://en.wikipedia.org/wiki/Hubble_Ultra-Deep_Field

lxx https://www.britannica.com/biography/Edwin-Hubble

lxxi https://en.wikipedia.org/wiki/Cosmic_microwave_background

lxxii

https://www.ctc.cam.ac.uk/outreach/origins/inflation_zero.php#:~:text=Accord ing%20to%20the%20theory%20of,several%20important%20problems%20in %20cosmology.

lxxiii https://en.wikipedia.org/wiki/Void_(astronomy)

lxxiv https://en.wikipedia.org/wiki/Supercluster

lxxv https://en.wikipedia.org/wiki/Observable_universe

lxxvi https://en.wikipedia.org/wiki/Speed_of_light

lxxvii https://imagine.gsfc.nasa.gov/science/objects/bursts1.html

lxxviii https://www.ucg.org/bible-study-tools/booklets/what-does-the-bible-teach-about-clean-and-unclean-meats/infographic-which-animals-does-the-bible-designate-as-clean-and-unclean

lxxix https://education.nationalgeographic.org/resource/paleoclimatology-RL/

lxxx https://education.nationalgeographic.org/resource/lithosphere/

lxxxi https://www.currentresults.com/Environment-Facts/Plants-Animals/number-species.php

lxxxii https://www.usgs.gov/special-topics/water-science-school/science/what-hydrology

lxxxiii

https://en.wikipedia.org/wiki/Genesis_flood_narrative#:~:text=Waters%20rise %2C%20all%20creatures%20destroyed.&text=All%20creatures%20destroye d.,-7%3A24%E2%80%938&text=Flood%20lasts%20150%20days%3B%20God, grounds%20on%20mountains%20of%20Ararat.

lxxxiv https://en.wikipedia.org/wiki/List_of_flood_myths

lxxxv https://arkencounter.com/noahs-ark/size/

lxxxvi https://en.wikipedia.org/wiki/Noah%27s_Ark

lxxxvii https://scripture4all.org/OnlineInterlinear/OTpdf/gen6.pdf

lxxxviii
https://en.wikipedia.org/wiki/Wyoming_(schooner)#:~:text=With%20a%20len
gth%20of%20450,known%20wooden%20ship%20ever%20built.

lxxxix https://en.wikipedia.org/wiki/Cubit

xc https://thewaymagazine.com/the-cubit-in-bible-times/

xci https://savvycalculator.com/length-to-beam-ratio-calculator/

xcii https://ourworldindata.org/how-many-species-are-there

xciii
https://en.wikipedia.org/wiki/Cretaceous%E2%80%93Paleogene_extinction_
event

xciv https://www.usatoday.com/story/news/world/2022/01/16/oldest-modern-
human-remains-ethiopia/6548811001/

xcv https://en.wikipedia.org/wiki/Mesozoic

xcvi https://en.wikipedia.org/wiki/Quaternary

xcvii https://en.wikipedia.org/wiki/Stratigraphy

xcviii https://en.wikipedia.org/wiki/Cambrian_explosion

xcix https://en.wikipedia.org/wiki/Law_of_superposition

c
https://en.wikipedia.org/wiki/Cretaceous%E2%80%93Paleogene_extinction_
event

ci https://en.wikipedia.org/wiki/Epic_of_Gilgamesh

cii https://www.discovermagazine.com/planet-earth/who-were-the-ancient-
sumerians-and-what-are-they-known-for

ciii https://en.wikipedia.org/wiki/Akkadian_Empire

civ https://www.whoi.edu/oceanus/feature/noahs-not-so-big-flood/

cv https://en.wikipedia.org/wiki/Holocene

cvi https://en.wikipedia.org/wiki/Mesolithic

cvii https://en.wikipedia.org/wiki/Occam%27s_razor

cviii https://en.wikipedia.org/wiki/Kepler%27s_laws_of_planetary_motion

cix https://en.wikipedia.org/wiki/Jeanne_Calment

cx Biblical numerology - Wikipedia

cxi https://www.biblicalcyclopedia.com/N/nephilim.html

cxii Augustine of Hippo - Wikipedia

cxiii Augustine: The Literal Meaning of Genesis – GeoChristian

cxiv https://www.ncei.noaa.gov/access/monitoring/monthly-report/global/202213#:~:text=North%20America's%20yearly%20temperature%20has,climate%20conditions%20across%20the%20U.S.

cxv https://keelingcurve.ucsd.edu/

cxvi https://www.bas.ac.uk/data/our-data/publication/ice-cores-and-climate-change/

cxvii https://www.nature.org/en-us/what-we-do/our-insights/perspectives/ipcc-report-climate-change/?gclid=EAIaIQobChMIz8DQ-ZDLgAMVQ4CGCh0w3ghYEAAYASAAEgK9C_D_BwE&gclsrc=aw.ds

cxviii https://www.catholiceducation.org/en/culture/catholic-contributions/transubstantiation.html

cxix
https://en.wikipedia.org/wiki/Synod_of_Hippo#:~:text=The%20Synod%20of%20Hippo%20refers,known%20for%20two%20distinct%20acts.

cxx https://www.vatican.va/archive/hist_councils/ii_vatican_council/index.htm

cxxihttps://www.vatican.va/archive/hist_councils/ii_vatican_council/documents/vat-ii_const_19641121_lumen-gentium_en.html

Made in the USA
Monee, IL
20 September 2023